WHO
IS GOD
IN THREE
PERSONS?

WHO IS GOD IN THREE PERSONS?

A Study of the Trinity

FaithQuestions SERIES

John R. Tyson

ABINGDON PRESS
NASHVILLE

WHO IS GOD IN THREE PERSONS?
A Study of the Trinity

Copyright © 2005 by Abingdon Press

Scripture quotations in this publication, unless otherwise indicated, are from the New Revised Standard Version of the Bible, copyright © 1989, by the Division of Christian Education of the National Council of the Churches of Christ in the United States of America and used by permission. All rights reserved.

Scripture quotations noted RSV are from the Revised Standard Version of the Bible, copyrighted © 1946, 1952, 1971 by the Division of Christian Education of the National Council of the Churches of Christ in the United States of America, and are used by permission. All rights reserved.

This book is printed on acid-free, elemental chlorine-free paper.

ISBN: 0-687-73991-8

05 06 07 08 09 10 11 12 13 14—10 9 8 7 6 5 4 3 2 1

MANUFACTURED IN THE UNITED STATES OF AMERICA

CONTENTS

HOW TO USE
WHO IS GOD IN THREE PERSONS?
A STUDY OF THE TRINITY

WHO IS GOD IN THREE PERSONS? A STUDY OF THE TRINITY explores the doctrine of the Trinity from the perspective of the Bible, tradition, and church history. It addresses such questions as the following: Is the Trinity a Bible doctrine? Where did we get this doctrine? What issues and questions have emerged in the life of Christian faith over the centuries? Who are the persons in church history associated with these issues and questions? What difference does the doctrine of the Trinity make in contemporary Christian life? What are the real issues at stake in the doctrine of the Trinity? What does the doctrine of the Trinity tell us about the deity of Jesus? about God? about the Holy Spirit? This book is for adults who want to know more about the doctrine of the Trinity and its implications for contemporary Christian faith and discipleship and who want to know more about the nature of God, of Jesus, and of the Holy Spirit as expressed in the doctrine of the Trinity. It is designed for use in any of three settings: (1) adult Sunday school, (2) weekday adult groups, and (3) retreat settings. It can also provide a meaningful resource for private study.

Sunday School: WHO IS GOD IN THREE PERSONS? may be used on Sunday mornings as a short-term, seven-week study. Sunday morning groups generally last 45 to 60 minutes. If your group would like to go into greater depth, you can divide the chapters and do the study for longer than seven weeks.

Weekday Study: If you use WHO IS GOD IN THREE PERSONS? in a weekday study, we recommend 90-minute sessions. Participants should prepare ahead by reading the content of the chapter and choosing one activity for deeper reflection and study. A group leader may wish to assign these activities. You may want to use the additional resources referred to in the chapters and in the appendix.

Retreat Study: You may wish to use WHO IS GOD IN THREE PERSONS? in a more intense study like a weekend retreat. Distribute the books at least two weeks in advance. Locate and provide additional media resources and reference materials, such as Bible dictionaries and commentaries, copies of creeds from worship resources, and access to the Internet. Tell participants to read WHO IS GOD IN THREE PERSONS? before the retreat. Begin on Friday with an evening meal or refreshments followed by gathering time and worship. Discuss Chapter 1. Cover Chapters 2, 3, 4, 5, and 6 on Saturday. Develop a schedule that includes time for breaks, for meals, and for personal reflection of various topics in the chapters. Cover Chapter 7 on Sunday. End the retreat with closing worship on Sunday afternoon.

Leader/Learner Helps

Leader/learner helps are located in boxes near the relevant main text. They include a variety of discussion and reflection activities. Include both the Gathering and Closing worship activities for each chapter and choose from among the other leader/learner helps to fit the time frame you have chosen for your group.

The activities in the leader/learner helps meet the needs of a variety of personalities and ways of learning. They are designed to stimulate both solitary reflection and group discussion. An interactive and informal environment will foster a dynamic interchange of ideas and demonstrate the value of diverse perspectives. While the readings may be done in the group, reading outside of the session will enrich individual reflection and group discussion.

Most of the chapters include further research options in the endnotes. You will enrich your learning by reading one or more of the listed resources.

The Role of the Group Leader

A group leader facilitates the Gathering and the Closing worship, organizes the group for each session, monitors the use of time so that adequate attention is given to all major points of the chapter, and fosters an atmosphere of mutual respect and Christian caring. The leader should participate fully in the study as both learner and leader. The same person may lead all the sessions, or each session may have a different leader.

INTRODUCTION

I remember the first time I heard a person cast doubt on the doctrine of the Trinity. I was a youngster who had just come home from primary school on a bright and sunny spring day. My mom was in the back yard picking laundry off of the clothesline. As we chatted about school, a car stopped in front of the house and a well-dressed man and a woman got out and walked up to greet us. "Would you like to know the truth about God?" the man asked. "Certainly," Mother replied, and smiled. "There is only one true God, and his name is Jehovah," the man continued. "The Trinity isn't even mentioned in the Bible." The smile faded from Mother's face, as she replied: "Automobiles aren't in the Bible either, and I believe in them too." Our visitors made a hasty departure as she staunchly refused to take any of their literature. For a young person it was a startling experience! As they left, Mother explained that these people were "Jehovah's Witnesses." They didn't believe the same way we do about God, Jesus Christ, and the Holy Spirit. In fact, Mother was right. Jehovah's Witnesses do not believe in the doctrine of the Trinity and do not believe in the full divinity of Jesus Christ.

In a recent article, United Methodist theologian, Geoffrey Wainwright, described the doctrine of the Trinity as the doctrine "where the church stands or falls."[1] No matter how ethereal or unrelated to real life the Trinity might seem at first glance, it is a Christian doctrine that we simply cannot do without. In the chapters that follow I intend to use Scripture and Christian history, as well as reason and experience to show the importance and cogency of the doctrine of the Trinity. The Bible not only *teaches* the doctrine of the Trinity, I believe that a correct, Christian understanding of the Bible *demands* the doctrine of the Trinity. We will see how the church honed, fine-tuned, and struggled for a correct understanding of the Trinity. I will demonstrate how deeply interwoven the Trinity is into Christian believing and Christian living. I invite you to think concretely about the Trinity and its importance for our faith. I will also invite you to experience how vital the Trinity is to Christian worship by sharing several of Charles Wesley's *Hymns on the Trinity* with you. These hymns, rare gems among the jewels of our Christian heritage, have not been published and probably have not been sung since 1767. If you would like to sing them, I have suggested in the endnotes some familiar tunes and some hymn titles associated with them. Almost all denominational hymnbooks have a tune index in which you can find familiar hymns paired with the standard tunes I have suggested.

We Christians are having quite a bit of conversation among ourselves about the propriety of using terms like "Father" and "Son" for referring to our God. A significant portion of the difficulty that many are having with this sort of "god-talk" is that it seems to infer that our God is male or masculine in gender. The Bible is very clear on this matter: God is not male or female. Our God is described as Spirit, love, and light. The Bible also uses images like rock, eagle, and fortress to help us comprehend God. Gender language is used of God because Christians perceive God as being a personal God. Human persons come with gender, and much of our intimate language about persons and personal relationships is gender-laden language. The Bible and Christian tradition have given us the words "Father," "Son," and "Holy Spirit" as being useful in our understanding and in our references to God, if we understand them aright. We will explore these matters further in Chapters 6 and 7.

This book may be used as a study guide for a class or small group or as an aid to personal reflection and spiritual growth. However you wind up using the book, it is my fervent hope and prayer that it not only clarifies some of the issues surrounding the doctrine of the Trinity but that it also enriches your Christian experience. I hope this little study will enable you to appreciate the triune nature of our God more concretely and to experience God more fully.

John R. Tyson

1. Geoffrey Wainwright, "The Doctrine of the Trinity: Where the Church Stands or Falls," in *Interpretation*, Vol. 45, No. 2 (April 1991), pages 117–32.

CHAPTER 1
WHAT DOES THE BIBLE SAY
ABOUT THE TRINITY?

Focus: This chapter explores scriptural foundations for the Trinity

Gathering

Read or sing the hymn below. You may also read the hymn as a responsive reading.

1. Omnipotent God,
    Eternal I AM,
   We publish abroad
    Thy wonderful name,
   We worship before Thee
    Who reignest alone,
   And prostrate adore Thee
    Three Persons in One.

2. Jehovah entire
    In each we confess,
   And gladly admire
    Thy mystical grace,
   The Persons agreeing
    To make and renew,
   To give us our being
    And ransom us too.

3. Begotten again,
    And born from above,
   We join in the plan
    Of infinite Love;
   Son, Father, and Spirit
    Our Saviour we see,
   And glory inherit
    Thro' faith in the Three.

4. To Thee on the throne
    We lift up our voice,
   In Father and Son,
    And Spirit rejoice,
   With anticipation
    Of purest delight,
   And all our salvation
    Enjoy in thy sight.[1]

Pray together: "Gracious God, Guide us as we study your holy Word. Give us direction, wisdom, and understanding so that we might come to a deeper understanding of you and of ourselves in relationship with you; in the name of our Savior, God the Father, God the Son, and God the Holy Spirit. Amen."

I remember the first time I painted my mom's back porch. I was a sixth grader; my dad was working on the railroad and so his daylight hours were spent at work. I had heard my parents remark that the porch really needed a fresh coat of paint before we could set out the summer furniture and begin enjoying it. I had helped to paint the porch several times, under Dad's watchful eye, and I felt ready to tackle the job alone. I did a pretty good job of getting most of the paint on the porch and quite a bit of paint on myself as well, but I also recall making one major mistake. I started at the wrong end of the porch, the end away from the stairs, and I wound up painting myself into a corner. I had to climb over the banister and jump down to the ground (about five feet!) to avoid walking on my freshly painted floor.

The doctrine of the Trinity is somewhat like that experience. It matters a lot where you start out. We need to start out with the Bible and the very clear assertions that the Old and New Testaments make about our God. Just because the word *Trinity* is not found in the Bible does not mean that the ideas that comprise our belief in God as Father, Son, and Holy Spirit are not firmly grounded in the Bible. Indeed, I would suggest that any person who takes seriously what the Old and New Testaments teach about our God will be "painted into a corner" by the doctrine of the Trinity; there will be no reasonable escape (climbing over the banister won't work this time). The doctrine of the Trinity is based on several basic and very profound biblical assertions.

Our God Is One

The Jewish morning prayer, called the *Shema* [shuh-MAH], reminds the community of faith: "Hear, O Israel: The LORD our God is one LORD; and you shall love the LORD your God with all your heart, and with all your soul, and with all your might" (Deuteronomy 6:4, RSV). When the Old Testament texts use the word "LORD" in this capitalized form, the translators are signaling to us that they are translating the personal name of God from the original Hebrew text. The personal name of God, which was revealed to God's people in Exodus 3:13-16, is represented by the four letters YHWH in the Hebrew Scriptures. It is without a clear English equivalent. Following the practice of the Jewish synagogues, modern biblical translators substitute the word "LORD" for God's personal name.

The personal name of God was revealed to Moses in the context of a polytheistic world, in which many gods and goddesses competed for people's attention and heart allegiance. So one important feature of the "oneness" of the God of the Bible is that the community of faith is told, as in the first of the Ten Commandments, "You shall have no other gods before me" (Exodus 20:3). God, our God, is the only "one" for us; there is an utterly unique and exclusive relationship between us and our God. This assertion is further reinforced in the *Shema:* "The LORD our God is one

> Read Deuteronomy 6:4-10. What does this Scripture say to you about God? What does it say to you about human relationship with God? Look at this passage in a variety of modern translations. Compare and contrast the various translations of this passage and what they suggest to us.

LORD." The only proper response to the uniqueness of God's Lordship over Israel is an utterly unique devotion toward God: "You shall love the LORD your God with all your heart, and with all your soul, and with all your might" (Deuteronomy 6:4). This quality of devotion rules out putting anything or anyone ahead of the Lord, and it labels anything short of this kind of utter devotion as "idolatry." While we are not tempted to fall down before gods made of

> In contemporary Christian life, what do people place ahead of or in place of devotion to God?

precious stones or metals, we are certainly tempted to follow gods of convenience; these are "false gods" that are easily controlled and who make no major demands upon our lives.

The "oneness" of God, as described by the Old Testament text, also implies that God is not divided. This emphasis was one of the remarkable ways in which the Hebrew faith was distinguished from the view of their polytheistic neighbors. In polytheism the wind, rain, storms, clouds, thunder, and all the other forces of nature were seen as faces of the gods and goddesses; primitive people saw power and mystery in these things and hence viewed them as divine. But in the monotheistic Old Testament faith, God is the great Creator, whose power and glory are seen in nature (*see* Psalm 29), but the power of God is not diffused into nature or divided into a hierarchy of greater and lesser gods. This means that "the heavens are telling the glory of God; / and the firmament proclaims his handiwork"

(Psalm 19:1), but neither the heavens (or the things in them) nor the earth (or the things in it) were viewed as being divine. In this context, then, to say with the Old Testament writer, "The LORD your God is one LORD" (Deuteronomy 6:4), is to say that our God is not divided. God is the great Creator; there is no power above God or apart from God.

Out of the recognition of the unique power and exclusive relationship that the Old Testament community of faith had with God came a recognition of God's utter uniqueness. As Israel struggled with faithfulness and "having no other gods before" YHWH, the great prophets taught the people that God is incomparable and utterly unique. The lesson was to be learned in the Exodus deliverance, as YHWH reminded wayward Israel: "I am the LORD your God, / the Holy One of Israel, your Savior. / I give Egypt as your ransom …" (Isaiah 43:3). Using the language of an ancient jury trial, and speaking in the first-person through the prophet Isaiah, God called his people to the witness stand: "You are my witnesses, says the LORD, / … Before me no god was formed, / nor shall there be any after me. / I, I am the LORD, / and besides me there is no savior" (Isaiah 43:10-11). Again and again God used the voice of Isaiah to challenge the idolatry of his day: "Thus says the LORD, the King of Israel, / and his Redeemer, the LORD of hosts: / 'I am the first and I am the last; / besides me there is no god'" (Isaiah 44:6). Or again, "Declare and present your case; / let them take counsel together! / Who told this long ago? / Who declared it of old? / Was it not I, the LORD? / There is no other god besides me, / a righteous God and a Savior; / there is none besides me" (Isaiah 45:21).

New Testament writers also affirm the "oneness" of God. Paul, for example, makes allusion to the *Shema* in 1 Corinthians 8:4, when—in the midst of a controversy about the propriety of eating food offered to idols—he writes: "we know that 'no idol in the world really exists,' and that 'there is no God but one.'" The Epistle of James offers a similar reminiscence of the *Shema* in James 2:19. Many of the New Testament's moving benedictions, like 1 Timothy 1:17, point us "to the King of the ages, immortal, invisible, the **only** God…" (bold added). The "oneness" of God

Read 1 Corinthians 8:4-6; James 2:19; and 1 Timothy 1:12-17. What do these Scriptures say to you about God and about our relationship with God?

describes the unity and the uniqueness of our God; this is the basis of the monotheistic view of God that is shared by Christians and Jews.

Our God Takes Expression as Father, Son, and Holy Spirit

Even a casual reader of the New Testament discovers that various passages refer to God as "Father" and other passages refer to Jesus Christ as "the Son," while still other passages describe the work of "The Holy Spirit." In a few instances, like the "Great Commission" in Matthew 28, all three aspects of God are brought together in one location.

> Read Matthew 28:16-20. What do the words *Father, Son,* and *Holy Spirit* suggest to you about the nature of God?

Terms like *Father, Son,* and *Holy Spirit* show some of the difficulty of speaking about God. God-talk is difficult for humans because God is so many things that we are not. We have almost no frame of reference with which to comprehend God's holiness, power, might, love, wisdom, righteousness, glory, and so forth. In order to teach humans about God, the biblical writers compare the invisible God to things we can visualize and comprehend. In this way, then, our God—whose nature is "spirit and truth" (John 4:23-24)—is described as "Father." To refer to God as "Our Father who art in heaven" (Matthew 6:7) is an analogy that should call to mind the life-giving, guiding, protecting, and nurturing roles that God plays in human life. But sometimes the same analogies that make some things clear also confuse other things; that would certainly be the case with the Fatherhood of God if one concluded that God is male or possessed the serious shortcomings tragically seen in some human fathers.

The second person of the Trinity, "the Son," is described in various ways throughout the Bible. In the introduction to the Gospel of John, one of the most elevated descriptions of the second person of the Trinity, we learn that the second person of the Trinity existed before all creation, was with God the Father "in the beginning," and was "the Word" through whom creation was spoken into existence. Aspects like eternal existence and cooperation with the Father in the event of Creation signal the full deity of the Word, and so also does the text itself: "the Word was with God, and the Word was God" (John 1:1). To refer to the second person of the Trinity as "the Son" (John 1:14) is not to diminish his glory; it is rather to point to the unique relationship that "the Son" has with "the Father." Human fathers and sons (as well as mothers and daughters) have special relationships, but the relationship between God "the Father" and God "the

Son" goes beyond relationships as we understand them. We are told, in John 1:17-18 (RSV), that Jesus Christ is the same person as "the Son," and the Son "is in the bosom of the Father." The New Testament Greek phrase that describes this reality (*monogenēs*) literally describes the Son as "the only one born out of " the Father. In our world, we are more accustomed to thinking of the mother carrying a child within her; so once again the God-talk goes beyond our experience of life and gender. In this case the analogy is given to tell us about the shared identity that exists between the one who gives birth and the one who is born. How often have we peered into a baby's stroller and spoken of a child having his father's hair or her mother's eyes? The phraseology of John 1:17-18 tells us that we should be able to gaze into the manger at Bethlehem and exclaim: "O! He's got his Father's divinity!"

> Read John 1:1-6, 14, 17-18. How do these Scriptures speak to you about the divinity of Jesus?

The New Testament offers ample testimony to the unique, divine sonship of Jesus Christ. It begins with the theological introduction of John's Gospel, through which the reader peers into pre-history to learn that the Word of God, as the second person of the Trinity, existed before time began; there he was, from all eternity, with God, sharing God's nature. We are then told that "the Word became flesh and lived among us, . . . full of grace and truth"; hence the apostolic writer reports: "we have seen his glory, the glory as of a father's only Son" (John 1:14). The angel announced the same truth to Mary, prior to Jesus' birth: "the power of the Most High will overshadow you; therefore the child to be born will be holy; he will be called Son of God" (Luke 1:35). At Jesus' baptism, the Father's voice thundered down from on high with the same message: "This is my Son, the Beloved, with whom I am well pleased"

> Form teams of two or three. Each team will read one or more of the following Scriptures: Luke 1:35; Matthew 3:17; 11:25-30; John 10:30; 14:9; or Mark 15:39. Make a list of what the Scriptures say about Jesus. Compare and contrast this to the Scriptures from John 1. How do they speak to you about Jesus? Share your reflections with the entire group.

(Matthew 3:17). It has become fashionable to suggest that Jesus, as he is presented to us in the Synoptic tradition, makes no direct reference to his unique, divine sonship; but the relationship that Jesus describes in Matthew 11:25-30 is directly comparable to Jesus' testimony about himself in the Fourth Gospel; for the Synoptic Jesus to say on the one hand, "All things have been handed over to me by my Father; ... and no one knows the Father except the Son" (Matthew 11:27) is tantamount to the Johannine Jesus saying: "I and the Father are one" (John 10:30), or "Whoever has seen me has seen the Father" (John 14:9). In fact, the Gospel writers expect that anyone who observed the Jesus-story would recognize his unique, divine sonship; hence Mark reminds us that even the Roman centurion who witnessed Jesus' death on the cross was forced to exclaim: "Truly this man was God's Son!" (Mark 15:39).

> What do you think of when you hear the words *Holy Spirit*? What do these words say to you about God?

The word *Spirit*, as it comes to us from both the ancient Hebrew and Greek, can be translated "wind" or "breath." These synonyms for *spirit* offer us a beautiful word-picture for this aspect of the triune God. No one can see the wind, and it blows where it wills; but you can catch the wind with the sail of a small boat and its power will move you across the lake; the same invisible force will pull a child's kite heavenward. No one can see the wind, but we can appreciate the refreshment of a cool breeze on a hot summer's day. And no one can see a person's breath, but we know that with breath comes life and without breath life ceases. In this same way, these synonyms for *spirit* describe the invisible, but powerful, refreshing, life-giving, presence of God. To call the third person of the Trinity "the Holy Spirit" is to say that this isn't just any "spirit"; this is the Holy Spirit of the Holy God. In the ancient languages *holy* means "separate," "distinct," "sacred," "pure," and so forth; that is to say, that the "Holy Spirit" is a distinct snd unique manifestation of the holy God.

The Father, Son, and Holy Spirit All Equally Share in the Divine Nature

Not only does the Bible alternately call the Father (Philippians 1:2), Son (Jonn 1:1), and Holy Spirit (Acts 5:3-4) "God" but it also demonstrates the divinity of each aspect of God in many ways. For example, the Bible teaches that each person of the Trinity has always existed, without beginning, and will continue to exist, without end. It boggles the human mind to try to imagine what it means for God to have existence both before and after time and history; but it is clear that both time and history, which are the warp and woof of human life, are simply features of the world that came into being with Creation and will go out of existence with the end of all created things. Psalm 90:1-2 tells us that the great Creator, God the Father, was God before the earth and world were formed: "from everlasting to everlasting you are God" (Psalm 90:2). The Revelation to John describes Jesus Christ as "the Alpha and the Omega," the one "who is and who was and who is to come, the Almighty" (Revelation 1:8). In a similar way, the writer of Hebrews describes the Holy Spirit as "the eternal Spirit" (Hebrews 9:14), through whom Christ is

> Read Psalm 90:2, Revelation 1:8, and Hebrews 9:14. Make a drawing or diagram that represents the eternal nature of the Trinity as represented in these Scriptures. How do you think about God's eternal existence?

Divine Attribute	Father	Son	Holy Spirit
Eternal Existence	Psalm 90:1-2	Revelation 1:8, 17; John 1:1-2	Hebrews 9:14
Holy	Revelation 16:5	Acts 3:14	Acts 1:8
All Powerful	1 Peter 1:5	2 Corinthians 12:9	Romans 15:19
All Knowing	Jeremiah 17:10 1 John 3:20	Revelation 2:23 John 16:30	1 Corinthians 2:10-11
Always Present	Jeremiah 23:24	Matthew 18:20	Psalm 139:7
Truth	John 4:23-24	Revelation 3:7	1 John 5:6
Love	John 3:16	Ephesians 5:25	Romans 15:30
Benevolence	Romans 2:4	Ephesians 5:25	Nehemiah 9:20

able to "purify our conscience from dead works to worship the living God." By describing each person of the Trinity as possessing eternal existence, the Bible asserts that each person of the Trinity shares fully in the divine nature and existence. This concept is reinforced further by the way Scripture attributes the same divine attributes or characteristics to the Father, Son, and Holy Spirit.

In many instances actions that are attributed to one person of the Trinity are also subsequently attributed to the other persons as well. This is still another way in which the Bible demonstrates that the Father, Son, and Holy Spirit are all equally divine, share equally in God's important activities and actions, and therefore share equally in the divine nature.

Roles of the Persons of the Trinity

The Father, Son, and Holy Spirit share equally in the divine nature and share the same divine attributes, and they perform different roles. The varied roles or "jobs" that the Bible describes within the Trinity suggest why Christians are willing to speak of our one God as Father, Son, and Holy Spirit. In the event of Creation, for example, it is the Father who speaks reality into existence, with the liturgical repetition of "Let there be ..." (Genesis 1:3-28). And the Word (*logos*), the second person of the Trinity,

Action	Father	Son	Holy Spirit
Creates the world	Isaiah 64:8; 44:24	John 1:3; Colossians 1:15-17	Job 33:4; 26:13
Gives life	Genesis 2:7	John 1:3; 5:21	2 Corinthians 3:6, 8
Resurrects the dead	1 Thessalonians 1:10	John 2:19; 10:17	Romans 8:11
Dwells in believers	2 Corinthians 6:16	Colossians 1:27	John 14:17
Makes us holy	1 Thessalonians 5:23	Hebrews 2:11	1 Peter 1:2
Creates fellowship	1 John 1:3	1 Corinthians 1:9	2 Corinthians 13:14, RSV
Has a will for us	Luke 22:42	Luke 22:42	1 Corinthians 12:11
Searches our heart	Jeremiah 17:10	Revelation 2:23	1 Corinthians 2:10

"was in the beginning with God. All things came into being through him, and without him not one thing came into being" (John1:2-3). During this same time "the Spirit of God was moving over the face of the waters"

(Genesis 1:2, RSV). In a similar way our redemption from the wages of sin and death and the renovation of our inner person is a trinitarian work: it is God as Father who "so loved the world that he gave his only Son, so that everyone who believes in him may not perish but may have eternal life. Indeed, God did not send the Son into the world to condemn the world, but in order that the world might be saved through him" (John 3:16-17); hence, God the Son is our Redeemer. Jesus promised his disciples: "The Holy Spirit, whom the Father will send in my name, will teach you everything, and remind you of all that I have said to you" (John 14:26b); this is the same Holy Spirit that Jesus promised would abide with his disciples and be in them (John 14:17b). The work of the Holy Spirit within Christians is to "convict" or convince them of sin and righteousness (John 16:8, RSV) and to guide them into "all truth" (John 16:13). Working within Christians, the Holy Spirit transforms our inner character by growing the "fruit of the Spirit" there (Galatians 5:22-24). Our creation and redemption is a shared work, in which each person of the Trinity plays a role; and yet each event and both of them are the work of one and the same gracious God.

The Mystery of God

There is always a significant element of mystery involved any time humans attempt to understand or speak about God. Diligence and a willingness to be taught by the Bible can carry us a long way when it comes to understanding who God is and what God requires of us. But diligence and study also have to be balanced by deep humility. We cannot and will not be able to understand God completely; we cannot and will not be able to explain God comprehensively. Hence, the question that Job's friend, Zophar, asked him could be our question as well: "Can you find out the deep things of God? / Can you find out the limit of the Almighty?" (Job 11:7). The obvious answer is "No." No human, Job included, can "find out the deep things of God"; there will always be an element of mystery and limitation when we attempt to understand God. In fact, each of the qualities of God surpasses human comprehension.

As God reminded the people through the prophet Isaiah: "For as the heavens are higher than the earth, / so are my ways higher than your ways / and my thoughts than your thoughts" (Isaiah 55:9). In the Bible the language of distance, "higher," "farther," is often used to express the qualities of God. We are told, for example, that our God is "high and lofty"

(Isaiah 6:1); the language of "height" is not so much about the geographic location of God as it is a way of describing God as one who surpasses or "goes beyond" the limits of human comprehension. The superlative qualities of our God (wisest, kindest, most powerful) should not cause us to refrain from trying to understand God

> Read Isaiah 55:6-9. What situations in contemporary life point to the mystery of God's ways? What makes you aware that God's ways are not our ways?

as well as we can, using the resources God has given us; but they should inspire a deep humility in us as we undertake that task.

In his famous sermon, "On the Trinity," John Wesley ranked the affirmation of the Trinity among the main doctrines of our faith. Wesley wrote: "... there are some truths more important than others. It seems there are some which are of deep importance.... And doubtless we may rank among these that [are] contained in the words above cited [from 1 John 5:7]: 'There are three that bear record in heaven, the Father, the Word, and the Holy Ghost: and these three are one.'" He considered the threeness of the Godhead and the oneness of the divine nature to be essential biblical affirmations. But he also added: "I do not mean that it is of importance to believe this or that *explication* of these [biblical] words.... I would insist only on the direct words unexplained, just as they lie in the text."[2] Hence, Wesley was willing to allow that a person who had scruples about this or that human explanation of the doctrine of the Trinity to lay those explanations aside in favor of the simple and direct affirmation of the biblical witness. Anticipating a second scruple on the part of his hearer, Wesley noted: "It is objected: 'Whatever becomes of the text, we cannot believe what we cannot comprehend. When therefore you require us to believe mysteries, we pray you to have us excused.'"[3] He retorted to this supposed objection by describing it as a "twofold mistake." "(1). We do not require you to believe any mystery in this, whereas you suppose the contrary. But (2), you do already believe many things which you cannot comprehend."[4] Wesley listed quite a number of examples to illustrate his second point: the sun, light, the earth, the existence of the human soul, and the human body. At this point John Wesley introduced an important distinction between the "fact" of biblical assertions and the "manner" in which we understand them: "... the Bible does not require you to believe any mystery at all. The Bible barely requires you to believe such *facts*, not the manner of them. Now the mystery does not lie in the *fact*, but altogether in the *manner*."[5] Using the example of light, Wesley wrote: " 'God said, Let there be light: and there was light.' I believe it: I believe the plain *fact*: there is no mystery at all in this. The mystery lies in the *manner* of it. But of this I believe nothing at all; nor does God require it of me."[6] Applying this distinction to the doctrine of the Trinity, he asserted that the "fact" of the doctrine was the biblical assertion that our God is "Three and One." But the "manner" for explaining these biblical assertions was another thing entirely, and John Wesley was willing to let those explanations live in the world of mystery.

Closing

Stand, form a circle and join hands. Sing stanza 1 of the hymn "Holy, Holy, Holy." Offer a "bidding prayer" in which you offer praise to each person of the Trinity at the appropriate places in the following prayer. For example, pray:

"Gracious God, we thank you for coming into our lives as Father, Son, Holy Spirit. We celebrate your majesty, eternity, and your magnificent wisdom. We revel in your holiness and your will-to-save. Let us offer praise and thanksgiving to the Trinity. God our Father, we praise you for creating us . . . [pause to allow others to join in]; God the Son, we thank you for coming into the world . . . [pause to allow others to join in]; God the Holy Spirit, we praise you for offering us guidance and comfort . . . [pause to allow others to join in].

All: "We praise you, thank you, and celebrate you, our one God, Father, Son, and Holy Spirit."

Notes

1. Charles Wesley, *Hymns on the Trinity* (Bristol, William Pine, 1767; the facsimile reprint edition published by the Charles Wesley Society in 1998, page 104). This hymn can be sung to the tune "Hanover," used with the hymn "Ye Servants of God."

2. Albert Outler, ed. *The Works of John Wesley* (Nashville: Abingdon Press, 1984), Volume II, pages 376, 378. Hereafter: Outler, *JW Sermons*, II.

3. Outler, *JW Sermons*, II, page 379.

4. Outler, *JW Sermons*, II, page 379.

5. Outler, *JW Sermons*, II, page 383.

6. Outler, *JW Sermons*, II, pages 383–84.

CHAPTER 2
WHO "INVENTED" THE TRINITY?

Focus: This chapter explores early Trinitarian controversies and Tertullian's development of the orthodox doctrine of the Trinity.

Gathering

Read or sing the hymn below. You may also read the hymn as a responsive reading.

1. The Lord, and the eternal Word
    We our Creator see,
  The Spirit of his mouth concur'd
    And gave the worlds to be:
  The Father, Son and Holy Ghost,
    God in three Persons One,
  Created that celestial host,
    And made our earth alone.

2. "I by myself the heavens expand,
    "And spread the earth abroad!"
  All things sprang forth at the command
    Of one Almighty God:
  That One Almighty God, Thou art
    The glorious Trinity;
  Make known the secret to my heart
  Reveal Thy love in me.[1]

What does reflection upon God's creation suggest to us about the Trinity?

Based on our study of the assertions of the Christian Scriptures, one clear answer to the question: "Who 'Invented' the Trinity?" should be: "No one invented the concept of the Trinity; this is what the Bible teaches." But in another way, it must also be said that the ancient Christians used Scripture, as well as the Christian tradition, and read these resources with reason and in the light of human experience to develop the terms and concepts we use to express and affirm the doctrine of the Trinity. It is also an important matter to remember that the early Christians developed their understanding in the midst of serious doctrinal controversies that threatened to destroy the church and the Christian faith. The doctrine of the Trinity was not formed in mystical solitude or idle speculation; it was forged in fires of controversy and hammered out in attempts to preserve the faith and the church that had been established by Jesus and his apostles.

Early Christian Writings

The Trinity appears in the writings of the Apostolic Fathers, though not in a fully developed sense. References to the Trinity are generally associated with liturgy, short confessions of faith, or baptismal formulas. The Apostolic Fathers refer to the Trinity in the practical life of the church, but not (generally) in a doctrinal sense. One good example of this appears in an early church document called *Didache* (ca. 95), which means "Teaching." It is a church policy document that was probably composed in Palestine near the end of the first century; it is called "The Teaching" because it claims to present the teachings of the twelve apostles on matters of

> Form two research teams. Team One will look up *Didache*, and Team Two will look up *Clement* in a dictionary of church history, in an introductory survey of church history, or on the Internet. Ask each team: How does your research influence your thinking about the Trinity? Prepare a report for the group.

Christian practice. The writer of the *Didache* reports: "[C]oncerning baptism, you should baptize this way: having given instruction in these things, baptize in the name of the Father, and of the Son, and of the Holy Spirit, in running water. But if you do not have running water, then baptize with some other water; and if you cannot baptize in cold, [then] in

24

warm. But if you have neither, pour out water three times on the head in the name of the Father, Son, and Holy Spirit."[2]

Another early example appears in the *First Epistle of Clement* of Rome, which was probably written around A.D. 95. The letter is full of references to Father, Son, and Holy Spirit, which make it clear that Clement thought of each of them as being equally divine. Trinitarian language in *First Clement* emerges in the form of an oath or confession: "As God lives, and the Lord Jesus Christ lives, and the Holy Spirit" (58:2). In a similar fashion the three persons of the Trinity are mentioned in association with the apostolic mission: they went out "being filled with confidence because of the resurrection of the Lord Jesus Christ, confirmed in the word of God, with full assurance of the Holy Spirit" (42:3). Each Christian is confirmed in his or her own calling in a Trinitarian manner: "Do we not have one God and one Christ, and one Spirit of Grace poured out over us—one calling in Christ?" (46:6). Hence, the writings of the Apostolic Fathers offer a practical and liturgical affirmation of the Trinity that was not always carefully nuanced from the standpoint of doctrinal clarity.

Looking at Jesus Through the Lens of Judaism

The early Christians, who lived just outside the pages of the New Testament and sought to shepherd local churches during the transition from the leadership of the apostles (all of whom were dead by A.D. 95), are called the Apostolic Fathers. They are called "Fathers" because they were pastors of local house churches or congregations. They are called "Apostolic" because in many instances they knew and had been trained by Jesus' disciples. One such person was Ignatius

> Look up *Ignatius* in a dictionary of church history or online. What does your research about Ignatius reveal to you about the early church and its struggles? about early Christian understandings of God?

of Antioch (d. 115) who had been taught by Peter and Paul as a young man. As bishop (head pastor) of the church in Antioch, Ignatius had been arrested for publicly preaching Christ. When he refused to deny Christ and offer sacrifice and homage to Caesar as "Lord," he was sentenced to death in the Roman arena. While he was being transported across the Mediterranean world to meet his death in Rome, Ignatius penned a series of seven letters to the Christian congregations he passed along the way.

These letters provide us with a remarkable window into the life, faith, and struggles of early Christians.

In addition to the serious external threat of imperial Roman persecution, the early Christians faced the additional (and perhaps more serious) challenges of false teaching and schism. A recurring area of danger and theological conflict was the divinity of Jesus, and the early Christians struggled mightily to continue to teach the truth about Jesus Christ as it had been proclaimed by Paul and the other apostles. Since most of the first Christians had been Jews before coming to faith in Jesus Christ, one of the persistent threats to a Christology that was faithful to the apostles came from the attempt to "fit" Jesus into the existing theological structures of Judaism. This did not reflect negatively upon Jews as people of faith, but did seriously compromise the early church's assertion of the unique nature and saving work of Jesus Christ.

Paul's Epistle to the Galatians (Chapters 3–5) evidences his struggle against "Judaizers," who attempted to force Christians to keep the circumcision, as well as the food and ceremonial laws of Judaism, as the basis of their reconciliation with God. Paul argued that these "works," as well as Jewish heritage itself, were of no importance in the matter of reconciliation: "Now it is evident that no one is justified before God by the law; for 'The one who is righteous will live by faith.'... Christ redeemed us from the curse of the law by becoming a curse for us ... in Christ Jesus the blessing of Abraham might come to the Gentiles, so that we might receive the promise of the Spirit through faith" (Galatians 3:11-14). The apostle Paul urged that Jesus Christ had fulfilled the death penalty that stands against every human, according to the Jewish law; hence, in his cross Christ had achieved what the law could not—the reconciliation of humanity to God. This salvation is to be received through faith in Jesus Christ and not through human efforts at righteousness (however commendable they may be). Acts 16:1-4 offers an illuminating example of how these kinds of tensions emerged in the early church. In that instance Paul circumcised his Gentile-born pastoral associate, Timothy, so that Timothy could work effectively among Jews and Jewish Christians; without circumcision they would not have received Timothy or his message. The

> Read Galatians 3:11-15 and Acts 16:1-4. What do these two Scriptures say to you about the tensions between early Jewish and Gentile (non-Jewish) Christians?

Judaizers provided the context in which Paul enunciated his famous doctrine of "justification by faith."

The writings of Ignatius of Antioch show that Judaizers continued to be a problem into the second generation of Christianity. A sectarian group of Jewish Christians called themselves the ebionites (from the Hebrew *ebed*, "humble servant"). They continued to "fit" Christianity into the theological structures of Judaism. Not only was salvation to be had through keeping the Jewish law, but the "law of Jesus" (such as the Sermon on the Mount) was added to it, significantly enhancing the moral rigor of Judaism; but ebionism still offered salvation by human works, not through faith in the grace God has revealed in the cross of Jesus Christ. Equally troubling to the Christians was the willingness of the ebionites to read Jesus Christ through the lens of Judaism. The Old Testament has no conception of the Word becoming flesh and dwelling among us (John 1:14); the closest it could come to a theology of incarnation (God "taking flesh") was to point to the role of a great prophet—who revealed God in a complete and ultimate manner. This means that Jesus was not thought of as God's Son, the second person of the Trinity, but was thought of as a righteous human being through whom God was revealed in a decisive way.

The ebionite understanding of Jesus preserved the Lord's humanity but lost his divinity. It was a serious threat to the doctrine of the Trinity that could not go unopposed. Hence, in his letter to the church at Philadelphia, Ignatius of Antioch wrote: "If any one preaches the Jewish law to you, do not listen to him. For it is better to listen to Christian doctrine from a man who has been circumcised, than to [listen] to Judaism from one uncircumcised. But if either of such persons do not speak of Jesus Christ, they are in my judgment but as tombstones and graves of the dead, upon which are written only the names of men." The deciding factor in a person's proclamation, then, is not whether they kept the Jewish law of circumcision, but rather whether they

> What is your response to the assertion "The deciding factor in a person's proclamation, then, is not whether they kept the Jewish law of circumcision, but rather whether they preached accurately about Jesus Christ"? Today's Christians do not argue about circumcision, but other controversial matters might get in the way of us "hearing" whether a person preaches accurately about Jesus Christ —what should we do?

27

preached accurately about Jesus Christ. Hence, Ignatius urged his readers: "I exhort you to do nothing out of strife, but according to the doctrine of Christ. When I heard some [people] saying, 'if I do not find it in the ancient Scriptures [Old Testament], I will not believe the Gospel'; on my saying to them, 'It is written,' they answered me, 'that remains to be proved.' But to me Jesus Christ is the ancient documents; His cross, and death, and resurrection, and the faith which is by Him, are undefiled archives of antiquity, by which I desire ... to be justified."[3]

Looking at Jesus Through the Lens of Greek Philosophy

A second challenge to the doctrine of the Trinity, as it pertains to Jesus Christ, emerged from an attempt to blend Christian teaching with the philosophy and world-view provided by Hellenism (secular Greek culture). One of the earliest examples of this tendency is found in the work of Cerinthius. He was a Jewish Christian who lived and worked in the first half of the second century. Cerinthius sought to combine Jewish, Christian, and Greek philosophical resources to create a form of Christian faith that would appeal to everyone, without forcing people to change their minds about Jesus or their views of salvation and righteousness. The early Christian writers record three particular heresies that were taught by Cerinthius: (1) a Greek world-view and a dualistic understanding of the world and human nature. This meant, for Cerinthius, that "spirit" was good, and "matter" was evil. Indeed, the Old Testament God ("spirit") who created matter ("evil") was a bumbling and minor deity. It also meant that the incarnation of the second person of the Trinity made no sense to Cerinthius; to say that "the Word" ("spirit" = good) "became flesh" ("flesh" = evil) "and lived among us ... full of grace and truth" (John 1:14) sounded like complete nonsense to him. (2) This meant that Cerinthius had to develop a nonincarnational understanding of Jesus Christ. (3) Hence, he argued that Jesus only "seemed" to have a human body; in point of fact he was a spirit-being. This meant that Jesus was God (and therefore "spirit"), not human flesh

> Read 1 John 2:18-24; 3:23-24; 4:1-6. What do these Scriptures say to you about the humanity and divinity of Jesus Christ? How do they contrast with the teachings of Cerinthius and docetism? What connections do you see with the doctrine of the Trinity?

("evil"), and was therefore "full of grace and truth." Cerinthius's Christology (his view of Jesus Christ) was called "docetism," which stems from the Greek word for "seems to be" since he believed that Jesus Christ only "seemed to be" a human being, who had a true human body.

The First Epistle of John offers several warnings about the coming of "antichrists" or false teachers: "Who is the liar but the one who denies that Jesus is the Christ? This is the antichrist, the one who denies the Father and the Son. No one who denies the Son has the Father; everyone who confesses the Son has the Father also" (1 John 2:22-23). The writer of the epistle seemed to be speaking of Cerinthianism when he wrote: "... every spirit that confesses that Jesus Christ has come in the flesh is from God, and every spirit that does not confess Jesus is not from God. And this is the spirit of the antichrist " (1 John 4:2-3).

Ignatius of Antioch also wrote vigorously against the docetist Christology because he rightly recognized that denying the true humanity of Jesus Christ has the effect of losing him as our true substitute on the cross; Jesus Christ cannot die for the sins of humanity, as a true substitute for us, if he is not one of us. Hence Ignatius wrote: "He suffered all these things for our sake, that we might be saved. And He suffered [them] truly, even as He also truly raised Himself up, not as certain unbelievers maintain, that He only *seemed* to suffer, as they themselves only seem to be [Christians]. And as they believe, so shall it happen to them, when they shall be divested of their bodies, and be mere evil spirits."[4] Hence, Ignatius believed that denying the bodily nature of Jesus' suffering, death, and resurrection cuts a person off from his or her own resurrection from the dead.

Looking at Jesus Through the Lens of Secret Knowledge

Gnosticism gets its name from the Greek word for "knowledge," so the gnostic Christians were those who sought salvation through secret and recondite knowledge. Gnosticism was an eclectic and synergistic movement that drew upon Christian, Hellentistic Greek, and pre-Christian ideas. It shared so many similarities with Cerinthianism that it might be said that Cerinthianism was a variety of gnosticism. The gnostics embraced the metaphysical dualism of spirit and matter that we met in Cerinthianism; they shared a deep ambivalence about identifying the Creator-God of the Old Testament with God Almighty, who existed as pure Spirit. The gnostic ambivalence about matter also caused them to have difficulties with the incarnation of Jesus Christ. Some gnostics, like Marcion (d. 156) followed a docetist or Cerinthian Christology; while others developed a more sophisticated "adoptionist Christology," in which Jesus was a devout human being who was taken over by God's spirit ("the Christ") at his baptism. Thus, Jesus Christ was a Spirit-directed man, who was used by God up until the time of his unfortunate death on the cross. Since the bodily suffering and resurrection of Jesus is of no importance to the gnostics, several of their gospels include disclosure scenes in which the "Christ spirit" leaves Jesus during the Crucifixion and tells the disciples the real "inside truth" about salvation. *The Acts of John*, an apocryphal work of gnostic origins, offers an excellent example of these disclosure scenes in which the Spirit "Christ" reveals the "real truth" about his death to the beloved disciple: "You hear that I suffered, yet I suffered not; and that I suffered not, yet I did suffer; and that I was pierced, yet I was not wounded; that I was hanged, yet I was not hanged; that blood flowed from me, yet it did not flow, and in a word, that what they say of me, I did not endure.... And so I speak, discarding the manhood."[5] By dividing the humanity and divinity of Jesus Christ into separate persons, the adoptionists (like the Cerinthians before them) completely undercut the apostolic Christian understanding of the cross and resurrection of Jesus Christ and the role those events play in Christian life and faith.

> How do you think gnostic teachings challenged the doctrine of the Trinity? How do such teachings affect Christian understandings of God's grace? How does denying either the true humanity or full divinity of Jesus Christ affect other important Christian doctrines?

Gnostic writers were strongly opposed by early Christian writers like Irenaeus of Lyon (ca. 115–202) in his book *Against the Heresies*; by Scripture, logic, and ridicule he pointed out the errors of the leading gnostic sects. Irenaeus recognized that undermining either the true humanity or the full divinity of Jesus Christ destroyed the apostolic doctrine of salvation. On this basis, then, he opposed the gnostics: "For it was incumbent upon the Mediator between God and humanity, by His relationship to both, to bring both to friendship and concord, and present humanity to God, while He could reveal God to humanity. For in what way could we be partakers of the adoption of sons [and daughters], unless we had received from Him through the Son that fellowship which refers to Himself, unless His Word, having been made flesh, had entered into communion with us?"[6]

Looking at the Trinity as a Logical or Chronological Progression

As we have seen in the preceding sections, the early Christians struggled with how best to affirm the relationship of the one God to Jesus Christ. Many of the apostolic writers simply called Jesus Christ "God," while others wrote of Christ in ways that affirmed his divinity but also distinguished him as being separate from God the Father, clearly affirming that God is one and then also asserting that the one God took expression as Father, Son, and Holy Spirit. One of the early attempts at resolving this matter was called (by its opponents) "monarchianism." Among the monarchians the "rule" of the one God took precedence over other theological assertions about the Trinity. While asserting with the apostolic tradition the divinity of Father, Son, and Holy Spirit, the monarchians saw the Father, Son, and Holy Spirit as three successive expressions of the rule of the one God; God was "Father" or Creator in the Old Testament, then God became the Son during the ministry of Jesus, and finally (after Pentecost) God guided the church by becoming the Holy Spirit. Subsequent writers have called this approach "modalism" because it asserts that the one God goes through three successive "modes" of existence. While maintaining the "oneness" of God, modalism sacrificed the genuine "threeness" of the Trinity by changing it into a logical progression of three successive modes of God's existence. Praxaeus, a Roman theologian (ca. 200), was one of the pioneers of this point of view; he was strenuously opposed by the North African theologian Tertullian (ca. 160–220).

> Why do you think the idea of progression through three modes of existence challenges the doctrine of the Trinity? What New Testament examples can you think of to call into question the modalistic conception of the Trinity?

Tertullian had a profound sense of the importance of what he called the "Rule of Faith," and this amounted to the apostolic teaching as it had been handed down through the decades by men and women of faith. One of the first writers to describe the contents of the Rule of Faith, Tertullian includes within it most of the assertions that would subsequently become the Apostles' Creed. He also had a very low threshold of tolerance for what he considered idle speculation, since Tertullian felt that most heresies came from mixing Christianity with this or that speculative thought form. As a result he was both opposed to idle speculation and he was opposed to mixing Christian doctrine with pagan philosophy. To this end, he wrote: "What indeed has Athens to do with Jerusalem? What concord is there between the Academy and the Church? What between heretics and Christians? Our instruction comes from 'the porch of Solomon' [Acts 3:5], who had himself taught that 'the Lord should be sought in simplicity of heart' [Wis.1:11]. Away with all attempts to produce a mottled Christianity of Stoic, Platonic, and dialectic composition! We want no curious disputation after enjoying the gospel!"[7]

Tertullian attacked Praxaeus's views in writing because they confused the threefold nature of the Trinity in an attempt to clarify the oneness of God. He showed that Praxaeus's views not only contradicted the clear teaching of Scripture, which asserts that Father,

> Look up *Tertullian* in a dictionary of church history, in a survey book on church history, or on the Internet. How does your research inform your understanding of the doctrine of the Trinity?

Son, and Holy Spirit are eternal (for example), but also resulted in bringing confusion to the doctrine of salvation. This literary attack upon Praxaeus forced Tertullian to come to terms with what the Rule of Faith taught about the Trinity and how that could be best expressed; hence, *Against Praxaeus* (A.D. 210) had the constructive result that it led Tertullian to develop the orthodox doctrine of the Trinity and some of the terminology that the Christian church has embraced ever since.

Tertullian Invents the Terminology for Expressing the Trinity

Quintus Septimius Florens Tertullianus was born in Carthage (currently Libya), North Africa around the year A.D. 160. Very little definitive information is available about his early life. Christian tradition has described him as the son of a Roman centurion and a Berber mother; he was well educated in rhetoric and the law and may have gone to Rome to practice law. There is a "Tertullian" cited in the Roman legal archives as a person who tried cases before the Roman Senate, but we have no way of knowing whether this was the same man who became the architect for the Christian doctrine of the Trinity. He was converted to Christian faith not later than A.D. 197. Christian tradition says that his conversion occurred in

Rome through contact with the early Christian academy established by apologist Justin Martyr (d. 165). We do know that Tertullian was back in North Africa by the year A.D. 200 and was serving as priest in the church at Carthage. The teachings of Praxaeus, which he had heard in Rome, and the divisions emerging in the North African church caused him to take a theological interest in the doctrine of the Trinity.

Tertullian is the first Christian writer to use the word *trinity*; it is generally assumed that he invented the term. *Trinity* is a combination of the Latin word for "three" (*tri*) and the Latin word for "unity" (*unitas*); to a Latin-speaking world it was a good way of saying, "Our God is three and one." But Tertullian also recognized that it sounds like nonsense to say that some one or some thing is three and one at the same time and in the same way. Many people have this same struggle with the Trinity today; it sounds like too much of a sacrifice of the intellect for them to say that 1 (Father) + 1 (Son) + 1 (Holy Spirit) =

> When we Christians affirm, with Tertullian, that our God exists in "three persons who have the same substance," what are we asserting? How does this assertion affect your understanding of God?

1 (God). First of all, this objection points out some of the difficulty of trying to pierce the mysteries of the Trinity; but it is also clear that this mathematical formula does not actually represent what the doctrine of the Trinity is saying. Tertullian made this matter a bit clearer by introducing two other new terms to the discussion of the Trinity. Borrowing a term from Roman law, he used the word *person* to describe the "three-ness" of God. When contemporary people hear the word *person* they are apt to think of individualism or the rights of individuals: "I'm a person just like you!" But in Roman law the word *person* described the "parties" that were united in a legal contract; hence, the emphasis of "God in three persons" was not intended to fall upon the separateness of three individuals, but rather upon the unity of three individuals. The third term that Tertullian introduced into his discussion of the Trinity was *substance*. This term also was borrowed from Roman law; it was used to describe the "substance" or significance of an argument or law. Modern people are apt to think of the chemical make-up of a material when they hear the word *substance*, but that is reading the term through the lens of modern science rather than through the eyes of Roman law. Tertullian used the word *substance* to describe the "oneness" or unity of the triune God; it

was a shorthand way of saying that the Father, Son, and Holy Spirit all have the same significance for Christians.

While Tertullian did not solve all the difficult problems associated with the doctrine of the Trinity, he did provide the church with the terms and distinctions that allowed Christians to express the doctrine more coherently and led to greater unanimity within the Christian community on this matter. He also resolved one of the nagging questions about the Trinity by asserting that Christians are not asked to sacrifice their common sense in order to affirm the triune nature of God. By supplying the church with the distinctions between *person* and *substance*, Tertullian rightly showed that in affirming the Trinity we are saying that our God is one in a particular way and three in another particular way. To recognize that the Trinity asserts that God is one in one way and three in a different way helps clarify this aspect of the Trinity (to some degree). Even human beings can, by analogy, be "one" in a particular way (substance) and yet also take on three separate (but united) expressions (persons); for example, the same woman can be a daughter, spouse, and mother all at the same time. While the human analogy does not adequately explain the Trinity, it does help us appreciate the logic of the distinctions Tertullian introduced into the conversation.

Closing
Stand, form a circle, and join hands. Sing stanza 1 of the hymn "Holy, Holy, Holy." Read the following Charles Wesley hymn in unison as a closing prayer.

One God Jehovah is the Son,
In union with his Father one,
One Shepherd He, the great the good,
Who dearly bought us with his blood:
The sheep we of his pasture are,
His people and peculiar care;
And all the plenitude divine
In Jesus is for ever mine.[8] Amen.

Notes

1. Charles Wesley, *Hymns on the Trinity*, page 71. Sing this hymn to a tune like "Carol," used with the hymn "It Came Upon a Midnight Clear," or "Forest Green," used with the hymn "I Sing the Almighty Power of God."

2. "The Teaching of the Twelve Apostles," in Roberts and Donaldson, eds., TANF, Volume VII, pages 379–80. Quoted in John R. Tyson, ed. *Invitation to Christian Spirituality: An Ecumenical Anthology* (New York: Oxford University Press, 1999), page 57.

3. Ignatius, "Letter to the Philadelphians," in Roberts and Donaldson, eds., TANF, Volume I, chapters 2–10, pages 79–85. Quoted in Tyson, *Invitation to Christian Spirituality*, pages 55–56.

4. Ignatius, "Letter to the Smyranaens," in Roberts and Donaldson eds., TANF, Volume I, chapters 1–9, pages 86–90. Quoted in Tyson, *Invitation to Christian Spirituality*, page 56.

5. Willis Barnstone, *The Other Bible* (New York: Harper & Row Publishers, 1984), page 420.

6. Irenaeus, "Against Heresies," in Roberts and Donaldson, eds., TANF, Volume I, Book III, chapters 18–19, pages 448–49. Quoted in Tyson, *Invitation to Christian Spirituality*, page 66.

7. Tertullian, "On Prescriptions Against Heretics," in Roberts and Donaldson, eds, TANF, Volume I, chapter 7, pages 246-47. Quoted in Tyson, *Invitation to Christian Spirituality*, page 64.

8. Charles Wesley, *Hymns on the Trinity*, page 10.

CHAPTER 3
WHAT DO WE KNOW ABOUT THE RELATIONSHIPS WITHIN THE TRINITY?

Focus: This chapter explores the unique relationships among the Father, Son, and Holy Spirit and how human relationship with each person of the Trinity influences daily Christian life.

Gathering

Read or sing the hymn below. You may also read the hymn as a responsive reading.

1. God was in Christ, th' eternal Sire
   Reveal'd in his eternal Son,
   Jehovah did on earth expire,
   For every soul of man t' atone:
   The one Almighty God supreme,
   Jehovah lavish of his blood
   Pour'd out th' inestimable stream,
   And reconcil'd the world to God.

2. The one, true, only God most high,
   Agent at once and patient was:
   As Man he did for sinners die,
   As God redeem'd us by his
       cross;
   Jesus the general debt hath paid,
   God in the Person of the Son
   Amends to God the Father made,
   For Son and Father are but One.

3. Father in Jesus reconcil'd,
   My Father if thro' Him Thou art,
   Acknowledge thine unconscious
   child,
   And hear his Spirit in my heart;
   One of the dear distinguish'd race
   For whom thou cam'st in
   Christ from heaven
   I languish for thy gospel-grace,
   I long to know my sins forgiven.

4. Thy Godhead whole was in thy Son,
   When Jesus pray'd and gasp'd,
   and died:
   The precious ransom was laid down
   'Tis finish'd; I am justified!
   The Spirit of faith applies the word,
   And cries thy new-born child to
   thee,
   Hail holy, holy, holy, Lord,
   One glorious God in Persons
   Three.[1]

What does this hymn say to you about the respective roles that Father, Son, and Holy Spirit play in our salvation?

Relationships are complicated matters, even on the human plane. The same relationship can be described in various ways, at different times, depending upon what core values we see in it. For example, a spouse can be a partner, a lover, or a friend; a parent can be life-giver, guide, protector, disciplinarian, and so forth. Describing the relationships of others can be even more difficult, so much more the case when they are not like relationships we have and the "others" under consideration are the persons of the Trinity. Various New Testament writers, most notably Paul and John, have given us significant glimpses into the inter-workings of the triune relationship of God. While we cannot and do not expect to understand these matters perfectly, we also believe that this instruction is given for our benefit and for our edification; so it behooves us to understand whatever we can about the inter-workings of the Trinity.

How do you define the relationship you have with a friend? parent? spouse? child? co-worker?

The Witness of Paul

The Pauline Epistles were "occasional documents" (with the possible exception of Romans) that were written to reply to particular problems in the churches Paul established during his missionary journeys. This means that the eternal Word of God comes to us through Paul's treatment of particular first-century situations. Behind the advice, encouragement, and exhortations of the apostle lurks a foundational Trinitarian theology. The organizational and structural presentation of the Trinity runs deeper than the occasional mention of Father, Son, and Holy Spirit in the Pauline Epistles and shows how deeply the Trinity was linked to Paul's understanding of the shape and function of Christian faith.

In First Corinthians, for example, he begins by describing himself as being called "by the will of God to be an apostle of Christ Jesus" (1:1, RSV). "God," in this case, seems to refer to God the Father, who draws people toward himself through Christ Jesus, God's Son. After a brief blessing, that celebrates two-thirds of the Trinity, "Grace to you and peace from God our Father and the Lord Jesus Christ" (1:3), Paul continues by thanking God (the Father) for the grace that has been given to the Corinthians "in Christ Jesus" (1:4). They have been enriched in the knowledge of God and through the testimony of Christ and hence are not lacking in any *spirit*ual gift (1:5, emphasis added). The whole Trinity is at work in the introduction to this epistle; the Trinity was at work in the calling of Paul and equipping him

> Read 1 Corinthians 1:1-5, 18-29; 2:10-16; 3:10-17; and Chapters 12–14. How do Paul's references to the three persons of the Trinity influence your understanding of God? of Jesus? of the Holy Spirit?

as an apostle, and the whole Trinity was at work in establishing the Christian faith among the Corinthians. This triune emphasis continues as Paul describes the "wisdom of Christ" (1:18-29), the work of the Holy Spirit, who "searches everything" (2:10-16), the foundation for our salvation that is laid in Jesus Christ (3:10-15), and the indwelling presence of the Holy Spirit: "Do you not know that you are God's temple and that God's Spirit dwells in you?" (3:16). The latter aspect of triune Christian life is further developed in Chapters 12–14, as Paul describes "spiritual gifts" (Chapter 12) and the "more excellent way" of Christian love: "And now faith, hope, and love abide, these three; and the greatest of these is love" (13:13).

Galatians begins in a similar fashion. Paul describes his office as an apostle as coming not from humans, "but through Jesus Christ and God the Father" (1:1); once again two-thirds of the Trinity has called Paul to his missionary vocation. His opening blessing (1:3-5) also joins the Father and the Son, as the apostle praises God for the salvation of the Galatians. After some autobiographical verses, in which Paul describes the independent character of his apostolic work, he moves into the heart of his argument: God's new way of bringing justification to sinners by faith in Jesus Christ. The last few verses of the autobiographical section set the stage for what follows: Paul describes his aim to "live to God," an aim that was not fulfilled under the law; but since he has been "crucified with Christ" (God's Son), "it is no longer I who live, but Christ who lives in me" (by the work of the Holy Spirit) (2:20).

The third chapter of Galatians focuses our attention upon the reconciling death of Jesus Christ, the second person of the Trinity. Through faith and through baptism the Galatians have become justified and reconciled with God: "As many of you as were baptized into Christ have clothed yourselves with Christ" (3:27). The fourth chapter of Galatians describes the bondage that is experienced by those who try to live by God's law, and in the first half of Chapter 5 Paul contrasts this bondage by describing the freedom that is available through Jesus Christ: "For freedom Christ has set us free. Stand firm, therefore, and do not submit again to a yoke of slavery" (5:1). Paul then gives a lengthy discussion of Christian life as walking "by the Spirit"; this includes not gratifying "the desires of the

> Read Galatians 5 and Galatians 6:1-10. How do these Scriptures inform your understanding of how to live and act as a Christian?

flesh" and following "what the Spirit desires" (5:16-17). The Holy Spirit, who dwells within Christians, creates Christians' character by growing "the fruit of the Spirit" in them (5:22-25). Once again, Paul's presentation of the Christian life begins with God the Father, evidences the cooperation of the Father and the Son in bringing about our salvation, and turns to the work of the Holy Spirit to describe the nature of Christian life.

A final example of this same Trinitarian pattern appears in Romans. Romans is considered Paul's most complete statement of his message because this epistle was written to a church that Paul did not establish; hence it has none of the practical circumstances that seem to predominate his more "occasional" epistles. In Romans, Paul is simply preaching his gospel on paper; and in this instance he begins exactly as he did in the preceding examples—he describes his apostolic office as being from God, through the grace of Jesus Christ (1:3-5) and then offers a greeting: "To all God's beloved in Rome, who are called to be saints: Grace to you and peace from God our Father and the Lord Jesus Christ" (Romans 1:7). Once again, two-thirds of the Trinity, God the Father and Son, play a cooperative role in Paul's description of his call and appear in his greeting.

The constructive argument of Romans also begins with God the Father as Paul describes, at length, how all humans stand under the judgment of God because of their sin (Romans 1:18–3:20): "For the wrath of God is revealed from heaven against all ungodliness and wickedness of those who by their wickedness suppress the truth" (1:18). The aim of this section is to show the utter futility of attempting to reconcile oneself to God through works of the law. Paul's succinct summary to this section rules this out: "For 'no human being will be justified in his [God's] sight' by deeds prescribed by the law, for through the law comes the knowledge of sin" (3:20).

In the second major section of Romans, Paul shifts his attention to the second person of the Trinity (Romans 3:21–8:1) as the apostle describes "the righteousness of God through faith in Jesus Christ for all who believe" (3:22). After showing that the way of reconciliation through the law amounts to a dead end and then describing the righteousness that comes to us by faith in Jesus Christ, Paul concludes his message by describing "the law of the Spirit" (Romans 8:2-30). Once again Paul describes Christian life as walking "according to the Spirit" (8:4) and gives one of his most extended discussions of life under the influence of the third person of the Trinity. Setting one's mind upon the Spirit is "life and peace" (8:6). Having the indwelling presence of the Holy Spirit is endemic to being Christian, because: "Anyone who does not have the Spirit of Christ does not belong to him [Christ]. But if Christ is in you, though the body is dead because of sin, the Spirit is life because of righteousness" (8:9-10). The inner presence of the Holy Spirit sets Christians free because they do not live in

> Set aside a quiet time and place. Prayerfully read Romans. What do Paul's words say to you about God, Jesus, and the Holy Spirit? In what ways do his words enhance your experience with the three persons of the Trinity? How do they inspire you in your daily Christian life?

bondage to an outer law, but are instead guided from within by the Spirit; hence they are no longer "slaves" but sons, daughters, and heirs of God. The Holy Spirit bears witness to the fact that they belong to God (8:15-16) by giving them the witness of the Spirit that enables them to cry

"Abba! Father!" and gives a profound sense of belonging to God. The Holy Spirit is, indeed, our Comforter, who groans with us as the whole world awaits adoption by God (8:23), and "Likewise the Spirit helps us in our weakness; for we do not know how to pray as we ought, but that very Spirit intercedes with sighs too deep for words" (8:26). In a similar way, the Holy Spirit bore witness to the truth in Paul's own conscience (9:1).

The Witness of a Christological Hymn

The second chapter of Philippians (2:6-11) has long been viewed as a portion of an early Christian hymn that has been embedded in the Pauline Epistle; in recognition of the poetic structure of this passage, several contemporary versions set this poetical passage off from the prose portion of the chapter.[2] It is as though the apostolic writer drew upon a popular hymn to express his theology and to establish a bridge of connection with his readers—to whom the hymn was probably also well known. Whatever the origin or structure of this passage, it is an important witness to the apostolic teaching about the relationship between the Father and the Son, especially as it pertains to the incarnation ("taking flesh") of the Son.

> Read Philippians 2:1-11. What do the words "Let the same mind be in you that was in Christ Jesus" (verse 5) suggest to you? How does this hymn describe the relationship between God the Father and Jesus the Son? What does it say to you about Jesus? What does it suggest to you about Christian life?

The first important assertion is that Jesus Christ was found in the "form of God" (Philippians 2:6). This is a reference to the pre-incarnate form of the second person of the Trinity (the Word), but yet it is clear that Jesus Christ maintained divine nature even in his incarnation. A very similar statement is made in Colossians: "He is the image of the invisible God, the firstborn of all creation" (1:15). That being found in "the form of God" amounts to saying that he had "equality with God" is made clear in Philippians 2:6, and yet this divine form was not something Jesus Christ "grasped" (RSV) or clung to (the NRSV says "exploited"); it was something he laid aside during the Incarnation so that he could take the form of a servant. If we ask, "of what did Jesus Christ empty himself?" (2:7), the answer is not his divinity, *per se*, but the prerogatives of his divinity. Jesus Christ went through human life, using human resources—he occasionally used his divine power to help others (as "a servant"), but he never used it to help himself. That Jesus' human nature was as complete as his divine nature is also asserted in the text: "And being found in human form, / he humbled himself / and became obedient unto the point of death— / even death on a cross" (2:7b-8).

In the Incarnation, the second person of the Trinity assumed human form in order to take upon himself the role of a suffering servant; it was a role that the Hebrew Scriptures had long attributed to the coming Messiah, and it is difficult for Christians to read passages like Isaiah 53:4-5 and not think that this passage was written about the saving death of Jesus Christ. And there is clear indication from the Gospels that Jesus understood himself as a messiah in the way predicted by Isaiah (*see* Luke 4:16-20). Because Jesus Christ was "obedient to the point of death," God (the Father) has exalted him above every other name: ". . . at the name of Jesus / every knee should bend, / in heaven and on earth and under the earth, / and every tongue should confess / that Jesus Christ is Lord, / to the glory of God the Father" (2:10-11).

> Read Isaiah 53:4-5 and Luke 4:16-20. Look up *messiah* in a Bible dictionary like *The Interpreter's Dictionary of the Bible.* What do the Scriptures and your research say to you about Jesus? about the relationship between God and Jesus? about the Trinity?

God the Father was so intimately involved in the Incarnation, reconciliation, and Resurrection of God's Son that giving homage to Jesus Christ is one and the same as giving glory to God the Father.

The Witness of Johannine Theology to the Father and Son

The Gospel According to John is generally considered to be one of the last New Testament books written. I think it is fair to assume that the theological heresy that was addressed in First John forms a part of the background of the Gospel. The writer issued several warnings about "antichrists" coming into the world (1 John 2:18). Since these people denied that Jesus was the Christ (1 John 2:22) and claimed to have fellowship with the Father even though they denied the Son (1 John 2:23), they posed a serious danger to the Christian community. Their false teaching might lead people astray; their rejection of Jesus as the Christ would almost certainly divide the community. First John 4 continues in a similar vein. Again the issue has to do with the proper understanding of Jesus Christ, and the writer claims to be an eyewitness to the Christ event: "We have seen and do testify that the Father has sent his Son as the Savior of the world" (1 John 4:14). On this basis, then, First John stresses the difference between true and false teaching: "By this you know the Spirit of God: every spirit that confesses that Jesus Christ has come in the flesh is from God, and every spirit that does not confess Jesus is not from God. And this is the spirit of the antichrist. . ." (1 John 4:2-3). This Christological heresy, which may have been early gnosticism or Cerinthianism, denied the Incarnation and that Jesus was the Christ or Savior sent from God. In these assertions, it clearly stood outside the Christian faith as it had been handed down from the apostles, and for this reason John probably wrote his Gospel to oppose it.

This opposition started with the introduction (sometimes called "prologue") to the Fourth Gospel. To say that "in the beginning was the Word" is to say that the Word is eternal, the Word existed before time and space came into being. To say "the Word was with God, and the Word was God" is simply to fill out the former assertion; the Word is an eternal being, that is to say the Word is God. When John writes about "the Word," he is using a philosophical concept that was common to Hellenistic readers; *logos* in the Greek. It means "logic, mind, discourse, word," or "the study of" something; this is not a static "word," like a noun or verb. In fact, when John Calvin, founder of the Reformed Protestant faith, translated this "word" (*logos*) for his New Testament commentary, he used the Latin word *sermo* from which we get "sermon" rather than *verbum*, which is used to describe "word" as a point of grammar. It is an instructive translation. We would do well to think of the incarnation of Jesus Christ as a "sermon" from God on the topic of God's nature.

Jesus' divine sonship is one of the persistent themes of all the Gospels, but it is most especially so in John. This Gospel describes God as "Father" more than a hundred times,[3] which is more than any other New Testament book and nearly as much as the rest of the New Testament. John clearly does not want his readers to miss this point: the eternal, divine Word is the *only* Son of the Father (John 1:14). We must stress the uniqueness of Jesus' divine sonship precisely because Jesus did. Certainly, there is a sense in which all humans are "children of God," but we are not referring to this general relationship with God when we speak of Jesus' divine sonship; it is something entirely unique. A close examination of the phraseology that Jesus used to describe his relationship with God bears this out.

The only instance in which Jesus speaks of "our Father" as though the disciples and he had the same kind of relationship with the Father is when he was teaching his disciples how to pray (Matthew 6:9), and Jesus specifically tells them: "[you] pray then in this way. . . ." When Jesus prayed to God he said, "Abba [daddy!], Father" (Mark 14:36), not "our Father." In Matthew 18:35, Jesus uses the word "my" when he speaks to his disciples about his relationship with the Father. In John 20:17, Jesus says "my Father and your Father," which communicates their unity in God the Father and which also signals that Jesus' relationship with the Father was on a separate plane than that of the disciples.

John's Gospel seems to go out of its way to tell us that Jesus enjoyed a unique relationship with the Father. There are direct statements from the Gospel in which Jesus says things like: "The Father and I are one" (John 10:30), or "If you know me, you will know my Father also" (John 14:7, 9), and "I am in my Father" (John 14:20). In more extended discourses we read that loving Jesus is the same as loving the Father and keeping his commandments (John 14:21-24), or to take the opposite point of view: hating Jesus is the same as hating the Father also (John 15:23).

> Read the prayer that Jesus offers in John 17. What does the prayer say to you about Jesus? about his relationship with God? What would news headlines and news programs be like if the desire expressed in verses 20-21 were a reality in our world?

Jesus' prayer for his disciples (past and present) in John 17 is a wonderful window into the relationship the Son enjoys with the Father. Toward the end of this remarkable passage Jesus prayed: "I ask not only on behalf of these, but also on behalf of those who will believe in me through their word, that they may all be one. As you, Father, are in me and I am in you, may they also be in us, so that the world may believe that you have sent me" (John 17:20-21).

The Son and the Father work together, through this unique relationship, to bring salvation and new life to humankind. As Jesus said: "My Father is still working, and I also am working" (John 5:17). It is in this sense, then, that Jesus said: ". . . the Son can do nothing on his own, but only what he sees the Father doing; for whatever the Father does, the Son does likewise" (John 5:19). In this extended passage (down through verse 24), we learn that both Father and Son raise the dead and give life, receive honor, judge the world, and so forth. Jesus submitted to his Father's will and direction, which was the same as his own will, for the salvation of the world. Hence, when Jesus said, "the Son can do nothing on his own" he was not saying that the Son is not powerful enough or confident enough to act alone; rather it is in accordance with God the Father's will that the world is saved, and Jesus willingly submitted himself to work with the Father to achieve the Father's will.

> Read John 5:19-24. What insights do you gain from this Scripture about the relationship between Jesus and God? about God's work of salvation?

In a similar way, Jesus, as the Son of Man was "glorified" by his own saving death, even as his Father was also glorified in it (John 13:31-32). The word *glorify* suggests more than one meaning. Obviously, it means giving glory and honor to someone; but in Jewish culture "glorifying God" often involved raising one's hands. Raising of hands—in this case— is merged with the picture of Jesus' arms stretched wide on the cross; when Jesus said: "Now the Son of Man has been glorified" (John 13:31), or "The hour has come for the Son of Man to be glorified" (John 12:23), he was talking about his impending death as seen from the standpoint of his saving grace. The relationship between the Father and the Son is so close that what affects the one affects the other (John 5:24-25, 26-27); the Father and Son work together to bring salvation to the world.

John's Gospel weaves Jesus' true humanity and full divinity together to form a whole fabric of Christian witness. Not only are we told that "the Word became flesh and lived among us" (John 1:14), but we see Jesus' true humanity emerge as he experienced weariness and thirst after a long walk to Samaria (John 4:6-7), as well as a profound sense of loss at the death of his friend Lazarus (John 11:35). Even his post-Resurrection appearances demonstrated his retaining human form; hence, "doubting Thomas" was urged to satisfy himself about the truth of the Resurrection by touching Jesus' wounded hands and side (John 20:27-28). John's Gospel seems intent upon answering the critics ("antichrists") attacked in First John. Not only does his Gospel teach and show us that Jesus is the Christ, the divine Son of God and Savior of the world, it also shows us that, even as the resurrected second person of the Trinity, Jesus Christ shares our humanity.

One of the distinctive aspects of the Christology in John's Gospel is the forthright manner in which Jesus reports his divine identity in the Fourth Gospel. If Jesus seemed intent upon keeping his identity a secret in the

Synoptic Gospels (Matthew 16:20; Mark 8:30; Luke 8:55-57; 9:21), the secret is certainly "out" by the time the Gospel of John was written. The seven "I am sayings" are among the Gospel's most evocative disclosures of Jesus' divine nature and saving work among humans.

The "I am" format was not unique to Jesus in the first-century religious world. Mythical revealors in the Greek mystery religions, for example, also used this metaphorical way of speaking. As presented in John's

Seven "I am" Sayings in the Gospel of John	
The Bread of Life	John 6:35
The Light of the World	John 8:12; 9:5
The Gate for the Sheep	John 10:7, 9
The Good Shepherd	John 10:11
The Resurrection and the Life	John 11:25
The Way, the Truth, and the Life	John 14:6
The True Vine	John 15:1, 5

Gospel, Jesus seemed to be aware that others may be calling themselves "the Shepherd"; so he stressed his exclusive character by saying: "I am the *good* (literally "true") shepherd" (John 10:11); others may be calling themselves "light," but Jesus is "*the* Light of the World" (John 8:12); others claim to be "life, truth," or a "way" to God, but Jesus described himself as "*the* Way, *the* Truth, and *the* Life" (John 14:6).[4]

Read each of the "I am" statements in John. Choose one that especially appeals to you. Illustrate it or write about it. What meaning does it have for you? What does it say to you about Jesus? about God?

Jesus' exclusive claims are registered in an even more dramatic way in John 8. When Jesus used the "I am" (subject) without any predicate ("you are what?") in John 8:58, he was using a form of expression that was without parallel in Jewish and Hellenistic religious literature. The setting in John 8 is as dramatic as the "I am saying" itself. Jesus had just dealt with a woman taken in adultery (John 8:1-20) and her self-righteous accusers. In this passage Jesus attacked the basis of the accusers' self-righteousness—their descent from Abraham. Their question, "Are you greater than our father Abraham, who died?" (John 8:53), shows that they had caught the gist of Jesus' argument. But they pressed him further: "You are not yet fifty years old, and have you seen Abraham?" (John 8:57). Jesus answered them in a manner that was completely transparent to people brought up in the Jewish faith: "Very truly, I tell you, before Abraham was, I am" (John 8:58). In using "I am" in this fashion, Jesus was taking upon his lips the personal name of God that had been revealed to Moses at the burning bush (Exodus 3:14); this name was considered so sacred by devout Jews that they never even pronounced it—lest they take God's name "in vain." By taking God's name in this fashion, Jesus was declaring that he was (is) indeed one with the God of the Old Testament; that his hearers understood this reference is clear from their reaction to Jesus' words: "they picked up stones to throw at him" (John 8:59). Stoning to death is the Mosaic law's prescription for blasphemy (Leviticus 24:16). They picked up stones because it had not occurred to them that, in Jesus' case, this way of speaking was not blasphemy—it was simply another profound disclosure of Jesus' unique relationship with God.

Closing

Sing stanza 1 of the hymn "Holy, Holy, Holy." Read the following hymn aloud as a unison prayer. Spend a few moments of silence in which you consider what God might be saying to you through its words. Talk about your insights with another person in the group.

1. A wonderful plurality
   In the true God by faith we see,
   Who hear the record of the Son
   "I and my Father are but One;"
   In different Persons we proclaim
   One God eternally the same.

2. Father and Son in nature join,
   Each Person is alike Divine:
   Alike by heaven and earth ador'd;
   Thy Spirit makes the glorious Third;
   Co-equal, co-eternal Three,
   Show Thyself One, great God, in me.[5]

Notes

1. Charles Wesley, *Hymns on the Trinity*, page 13. This Charles Wesley hymn is based on the Scripture text of 2 Corinthians 5:19. It can be sung to "Candler," used with the hymn "Come, O Thou Traveler Unknown," or "Sweet Hour," used with "Sweet Hour of Prayer."

2. *The New International Version* and the *New Revised Standard Version* are among these.

3. William J. La Due, *The Trinity Guide to the Trinity* (Harrisburg: Trinity Press International, 2003), page 20.

4. Emphasis added.

5. Charles Wesley, *Hymns on the Trinity*, page 14. This hymn is based on John 10:30. Sing it to a tune like "St. Catherine," used with the hymn "Faith of Our Fathers," or "Selena," used with the hymn "O Love Divine, What Hast Thou Done."

CHAPTER 4
WHY SUCH A BIG DEBATE ABOUT A SMALL LETTER ("i")?

Focus: This chapter explores the Arian debate, the Council of Nicea, and the Nicene Creed.

Gathering

Read or sing the hymn below. You may also read the hymn as a responsive reading.

1. The Sovereign Lord of hosts
     is one,
   For ever glorified,
   The First and the Last is God
     alone,
   There is no God beside:
   Worship divine to Him is due,
     Who doth the title claim,
   The Alpha and Omega too,
     The First and Last I AM.

2. The King of Saints, the Lord
     of hosts,
   Almighty to redeem,
   In Him his ransom'd people trusts
     The one great God supreme:
   Jesus, Thou art to us made known
     Fulness of Deity:
   There is no other God but one,
     No other God but Thee.[1]

What do these verses say to you about the divinity of Jesus Christ?

Two epoch-making events occurred in the early decades of the fourth century, both of which had lasting impact upon the Christian church. The first of these, and by far the most far-reaching, was the conversion of the Roman emperor Constantine during his rise to power. In A.D. 312, on the eve of an important battle, as Constantine's troops marched on Rome to take control of the Roman Empire, he had a vision in which he was shown the Greek letters *Chi* and *Rho* set against the disk of the sun. *Chi* and *Rho* are the first two letters of "Christ" in Greek, and their imposition upon the sun formed the shape of a cross. A voice, in his vision, told Constantine: "By this sign you shall conquer." A devout sun worshiper, he took this as an omen from God and had his troops emblazon the *Chi-Rho* on their shields the next morning. At the battle of the Milvan Bridge Constantine's forces won a resounding victory, and he assumed the Imperial throne.

The depth of Constantine's Christianity has been a matter of significant debate down through the ages. He was sincere enough to put an end to persecution, to endow Bibles and churches, and to build great cathedrals. Under his rule Christianity went from the catacombs and cellars to occupy huge public edifices; it went from being persecuted nearly into extinction to becoming the most privileged among all the religions of the Roman world. Yet, Constantine's Christianity had enough superstition mixed in it for him to put off being baptized till he was on his deathbed. It is also clear that there was some political acumen at work in Constantine's conversion. As a Christian, he did away with the notion of imperial divinity; where former Roman emperors had claimed to

> What connections do you see between religion and politics in the story of Constantine's conversion? What difference does it make that Constantine considered himself to be "devout" rather than "divine"?

be divine as a way of unifying their vast imperial holdings and to exact complete obedience from their subjects, Constantine saw that this approach was failing and he took another route. As the first Christian emperor, he was not divine but devout, and his newfound faith became the glue that held Constantine's empire together. With God up in heaven, and Constantine on the throne—by God's good pleasure—he need not brook opposition from other would-be emperors. And Christian leaders, like Eusebius of Caesarea, the first great church historian, were so supportive of his reign that they hailed Constantine's Christianized Roman Empire as the kingdom of God come upon the earth.

50

This brings us to the second epoch-making event of this same time period; the rise of Arianism. Constantine had given up imperial divinity, in favor of Christianity, intending to use Christian faith as the glue to hold his empire together; imagine his surprise when he found out that the Christians were not very unified. In fact, as he came to power one of the most serious theological threats to Christian unity was sowing seeds of dissension throughout the eastern (Greek-speaking) region of his empire.

The Rise of Arianism

Arius (ca. 250–336) was a pastor in the Christian community in Alexandria, Egypt. He was a very popular preacher and hymn writer, who used his musical talents to communicate in song what he preached in his sermons. The bishop of the same city was a man named Alexander. In 318, the doctrine of the Trinity had become a point of contention in the Alexandrian church. Bishop Alexander preached a sermon on the Trinity that was designed to set the matter to rest, but instead it increased the controversy. Arius became convinced that what had been preached was "polytheism of the Trinity." Perhaps in stressing the uniqueness and equality of the Father, Son, and Holy Spirit Alexander had stressed the distinction of the three persons at the expense of their oneness in the Godhead; at any rate, the sermon caused Arius to try to resolve the problem by developing a new way of speaking about the Trinity.

The focus of Arius's interest was the relationship between the Father and the Son, and he became fixated upon John 1:18, which uses the Greek word *monogenēs* to describe Jesus as the "begotten" or "only born" Son of the Father. We have considered the metaphorical character of this passage in a previous section, as we mused about what it means to say that

> Look up *Arius* in a dictionary of church history, on the Internet, or in another easily accessible source. How does your research help you understand God? Jesus? the Trinity? Talk about the results of your research with others in the group.

God the Father gives birth to ("begets") the Son. In our earlier discussion, we suggested that the point of the image was to stress that the Father and Son share the same nature and divine identity. It is as though we met on the street, and I said to you: "I see that you are a human being, I'll bet your parents were human beings too." My kids would call that assertion a "no-

> Read John 1:18. How does the Scripture speak to you about the divinity of Jesus?

brainer" and then make the sound "Du-ah!"—which when translated means: "that is pretty obvious." But Arius decided to read the old analogy a new way. He reasoned that if the Son is "begotten" out of the Father, then there is a time when the Father existed and the Son did not exist. Or to use another contemporary analogy: looking at you, and recognizing that you are alive, I could say to you: "I'll bet there was a time when your parents existed, but you did not exist." Another "no-brainer," but it gets a completely different meaning out of the biblical analogy of the Father "begetting" the Son. The focus of our attention is shifted away from the assertion of a shared divine nature, and turns instead to the question: "Who existed first?" Based on this analogy, the answer also seemed obvious; the Father existed before the Son. But is that really what the Bible intended to say with this analogy, or is it simply a conclusion that came from Arius's fertile imagination?

The implications Arius drew from his reading of the analogy showed, based on other Bible passages, that he was reading the analogy wrongly. For exam-

> What is your response to Arius's interpretation?

ple, Arius concluded that the Father was eternal, and therefore God; but the Son was not as eternal as the Father, and therefore was not divine or was not divine in the same way that the Father was. Arius concluded that the Father was eternal and uncreated and the Son was not eternal and was created.

A few people in the Alexandrian church, notably a man named Athanasius, recognized the wrong-headedness of Arius's solution to the problem of the Trinity and began to challenge Arius's theology. In a letter to one of his sympathizers, written in A.D. 321, Arius complained of the persecution he and his followers received for their views. It also offers an apt summary of Arianism: "We are persecuted because we say that the Son has a beginning, but God is without beginning. For that reason we are persecuted. . . ."[2] In teaching that the Son was a creature, who was subordinate to the Father, Arius asserted that the Son was not co-eternal (equally eternal) nor co-essential (of the same essence) as the Father. He redefined the nature of the Son's divinity to fit these new assertions. Arius believed that the Son's obedience to the Father was so complete that it allows us to think of the Son as being divine. In other words, the Son was so holy, that we could think of him as being the Holy One.

It is clear that Arius had redefined how the Christian church had always thought of divinity; divinity had always been considered the highest qual-ity of existence, and in this sense humanity and divinity were worlds apart. Humanity was one thing, and divinity was another thing. Lots of good humanity did not add up to divinity. The fallacy of Arius's theology could be demonstrated with apples and

> What intrigues you or challenges you about the issues of the humanity and divinity of Jesus? Why do you think the issues of quantity versus quality would make a difference in talking about humanity and divinity?

oranges. Traditional Christian theology has always taught that humanity and divinity were different things, like apples and oranges; but Arius sug-gested that a whole lot of good apples could be the same as oranges. Or to say the same thing in a more specific way; divinity has always been a dis-tinct *quality* in Christian thought, and Arius changed *divinity* into mean-ing a large *quantity* of holiness. The obvious implication of this line of argument is somewhat shocking: if by his holy obedience to God the Father, Jesus Christ became divine, then the same avenue is open to you or me as well. In this same way, Arius was willing to say that Jesus was "divine" (godly) but not Deity (God).

The implications of the Arian remaking of the Trinity were many but several are worth noting: (1) the real essential divinity of the second per-son, Jesus Christ is lost; (2) there really is not a Trinity because the Father and Son are not equal—Arius's view gives us more of a monarchy under the rule of God the Father than a Trinity, and (3) the Christian theology of salvation (*soteriology*) by God's grace is turned into a theology of works. It is as the divine Son of God that Jesus Christ is our perfect mediator on the cross. It is as true God that Jesus Christ represents God to us; and it is as a real human that he represents fallen humanity before God, both ele-ments of Christ's dual nature must be true for his death to avail our salva-tion, by faith. Arius could urge us to live like Jesus, or to obey God the Father as Jesus did; but he cannot speak meaningfully to us about the sav-ing significance of Good Friday or the transforming reality of Easter.

Enter Athanasius

Athanasius (ca. 296–373) was a deacon in the church of Alexandria, Egypt when Arius began his innovative approach to the doctrine of the

Trinity. He emerged as one of Arius's chief opponents both in Alexandria and across the eastern (Greek-speaking) part of the Roman Empire. In 318, he penned *On the Incarnation*, which, although it was written as a reply to Arius, would become one of the classic descriptions of how Jesus Christ's unique nature (as God and human) was necessary for the apostolic understanding of Christian salvation. The foundational premise of the work was exactly what Arius denied.

> Look up *Athanasius* in a dictionary of church history, online, or in another easily accessible resource. How does your research inform your understanding of God? Jesus? the Trinity? Talk about the results of your research with others in your group.

the Father and the Son, which was exactly what Arius denied.

On the Incarnation is a very extensive work, but the gist of Athanasius's argument is quite simple. It can be reduced to three logical steps: (1) the Bible teaches that only God can save; (2) the Bible teaches that Jesus Christ saves (Matthew 1:21; Luke 2:11); therefore, (3) Jesus Christ is God. This assertion is further documented by the fact that Scripture urges Christians to worship Jesus and to pray to God in Jesus' name (John 14:13-14; 16:23-24; Acts 7:59; 1 Corinthians 1:2-3); these acts would be utter blasphemy—unless Jesus Christ were truly God.

Along the way, Athanasius also gave expression to the classical explanation of the Atonement (saving significance) of Jesus' death: "Hence [the Word] did away with death for all who are like him by the offering of a substitute. For it was reasonable that the Word, who is above all, in offering his own temple and bodily instrument as a substitute-life for all, fulfilled the liability in his death, and thus the incorruptible Son of God, being associated with all mankind by likeness to them, naturally clothed all with incorruption in the promise concerning the resurrection."[3] That is to say, the full deity and true humanity of the Word of God, the second person of the Trinity, both were absolutely essential to the apostolic understanding of salvation. Athanasius emerged as the champion of Christian "orthodoxy" (true teaching), in large part because he was an able student of the Bible and Christian theology and because he was a pastor who had the keen

> Read aloud Matthew 1:21; Luke 2:11; John 14:13-14; 16:23-24; Acts 7:59; 1 Corinthians 1:2-3. How do these Scriptures inform your understanding of the divinity of Jesus?

insight to see what implications Arius's "solution" had for the Christian doctrine of salvation.

The Council of Nicea

Bishop Alexander had reviewed Arius's doctrine and taken council with him both in private and publicly. He was clear in his own mind that Arius's teaching was heresy, and when Arius would not recant his views, he was "silenced" and barred from ministry in the church. Leaving Egypt, Arius relocated in Nicomedia, in the court of his friend and supporter Bishop Eusebius; from that location he popularized his views and even gained influence at the imperial court through Eusebius's close association with Constantine's sister Constantia.

Constantine soon became aware of the division that was occurring in the church over Arianism, and he dispatched his most trusted religious advisor, Hosius, Bishop of Cordova, with instructions to mediate the dispute and reconcile the warring parties. But Hosius's missions to Alexandria and Nicomedia were futile. The dispute had gone too far to be settled amicably; there had been too many "anathemas" and denunciations, and there had even been bloodshed in the streets as opposing adherents entered into riotous conflict.

Constantine decided to take more direct action to quell the situation. At the prompting of several bishops, he agreed to call a church council to decide the Arian question as well as other nagging matters (such as the proper date to celebrate Easter). The council would be held in Nicea, in modern day Turkey, in A.D. 325.

> Look up *The Council of Nicea* in a dictionary of church history, online, or in another easily accessible resource. How does your research inform your understanding of God? Jesus? the Trinity? Talk about the results of your research with others in your group.

Nearly two thousand invitations were sent out, one to every bishop and abbot in the entire Roman Empire. Fewer than 400 bishops and abbots attended, in part perhaps because travel was so difficult; but it must also be said that the memory of imperial persecution was still fresh in the minds of many (it had only ended in 303) and to many it probably sounded too much like a trap. Christian tradition says that roughly 300 bishops (or 318 in another account) were in attendance, and each of these brought presbyters and deacons along with them. Most of these representatives came from the eastern part of the empire. The emperor addressed the assembly and greeted them warmly, but there could be no mistaking his intention for the meeting: "I rejoice to see you here, yet I should be more pleased to see unity and affection among you. I entreat you, therefore, beloved ministers of God, to remove the causes of dissension among you and establish peace."[4]

Many of the delegates were not strongly committed to either the Arian or anti-Arian position, so a considerable amount of the discussion amounted to both parties trying to win over enough of the "uncommitted" delegates to gain a majority. This process went ahead through presentations of position papers, which usually took the form of sermons, and creeds, as well as liturgies, hymns, and other acts of worship. Arius had been invited to attend the council, to present his own case, which he did amidst a series of chants and songs set to popular Alexandrian tunes. When Athanasius or another delegate presented the Arians with a tightly reasoned theological argument, they would respond by striking up the band and chanting another hymn.

The word *creed* comes from the Latin word *credo*, which means "I believe." Creeds have long been used in Christian communities as shorthand, liturgical summaries of the faith and as teaching devices in the community of faith. The first creed presented before the council had been drafted by eighteen Arian bishops. While it was careful to use biblical phrases, it presented the Arian position in such an exaggerated form that a riot nearly broke out in the meeting as it was read. One of the moderates in the group, Eusebius of Caesarea, put forward an alternative creed that had long been in use in his church. It began with the words, "We believe in one God, the Father Almighty, maker of all things visible and invisible." This creed would form the skeleton upon which the Nicene Creed would be fleshed out. The emperor liked Eusebius's creed and threw his support behind it. The Arians saw nothing in it that undercut their position, so they did not oppose it. The anti-Arians, however, recognized that the unaltered creed did not represent a genuine solution to the Arian problem; it only papered over the differences by giving the appearance of una-

> Read the Nicene Creed in the appendix of this book. What does the creed say to you about God? Jesus? the Holy Spirit? In what specific ways does the creed answer the Arian question?

nimity where there was none. Bishop Alexander and Athanasius had urged the addition of the words "of the same substance (*homoousios*) as the Father" as a bulwark against Arianism. The anti-Arians retired to draft a stronger version of the creed, which they submitted through Bishop Hosius. It contained the "of the same substance as the Father" (*homo*=same, *ousios*=substance) passage. Emperor Constantine and the majority of the bishops were willing to accept this as a true description of the relationship of the nature of the Son to the nature of the Father, only the Arians were unwilling to accept the *homoousios* phraseology. They argued instead for the term *homoiousios*, which differed from the orthodox creed merely by one letter—"i". Where *homo* means "the same," *homoi* means "similar" but not "the same." In this case, the old adage, "A miss is as good as a mile," holds true. Either Jesus Christ is equally divine with God the Father, or he is not; there is no middle way, and there can be no equivocation. Hence, to say that the Son is of "similar" substance as the Father was not good enough for the anti-Arians; they had gathered the necessary majority, prayers were said, the vote was taken, and the Arians were soundly defeated (one source says 312 to 4). They were given opportunity to ascribe to the Nicene Creed (*see* Appendix A), and when they refused the Arians were exiled from the church as heretics and dispensers of false teaching.

The historic Christian creeds served a variety of functions in the early church. They were liturgical devices, to be used for teaching in corporate worship; hence, many of them have a rhythm and nearly poetical sound to them. They were used as professions of faith, to be recited when a person joined a congregation. And they were used as teaching devices for the young, so that they would grow up in the teachings of the apostolic faith having heard them recited and explained year after year. With the

> What creeds do you hear or read during worship in your church? What is your favorite creed? Why? How does the creed connect to your understandings of God? of Jesus? of the Holy Spirit?

Council of Nicea, Christian creeds also took on a more overtly theological role in distinguishing true doctrine from false doctrine.

The Forgotten Member of the Trinity

While all this discussion about the divinity of Jesus Christ, the second person of the Trinity, and the relationship between the Father and the Son was going on, few people seemed to have noticed that precious little had been said about the place of the Holy Spirit in the doctrine of the Trinity. Indeed, one of the early versions of the Nicene Creed described the third person of the Godhead simply by affirming "We believe … also in the Holy Spirit." After the Council of Nicea, however, a group of very able Christian pastor-theologians began to explore and articulate the role of "the forgotten member of the Trinity."

> Why is the Holy Spirit so often "the forgotten member of the Trinity"? How can we be more attentive to the Holy Spirit? How important is the Holy Spirit to your Christian life?

Three men and one woman, Macrina, comprised a group of fourth-century Christian theologians called "the Cappodocians" after the region in which they lived *(see* 1 Peter 1:1). They were Basil, bishop of Caesarea (330–379), his younger brother Gregory, bishop of Nyssa (ca. 335–394), and their friend Gregory, bishop of Nazianzus (d. 390). They defended and delineated the apostolic understanding of the Trinity throughout the fourth century. Macrina (327–79) "the younger" was the sister of Basil and Gregory of Nyssa, and she wrote significantly on immortality and resurrection but did not contribute much to the development of the doctrine of the Trinity.

Powerful opponents to the apostolic understanding of the Holy Spirit emerged between the councils of Nicea (325) and Constantinople (381), and the Cappadocians opposed them by stressing the full deity of the Holy Spirit. While continuing to defend orthodox Christology, which had been established at Nicea, they also continued to preach and write against Arianism. Indeed, Gregory of Nyssa was forced into the fray over the doctrine of the Trinity at the Council of Constantinople in 381, just as Athanasius had been half a century earlier at the Council of Nicea. One instance of this false teaching occurred when Macedonius was bishop of Constantinople (341–360). He taught that the Holy Spirit was a "minister and servant of God," which seemed to place the Holy Spirit on the level of the angels and not squarely in the Trinity as one who is co-equal, co-essential, and co-eternal with the Father and the Son. Macedonius was opposed, both in person and in writing, by Gregory of Nyssa. In his *Against Macedonius,* Gregory described the Father, Son, and Holy Spirit as three torches: the first imparts its light to the second, and the second imparts its light to the third, and in this way all three persons share in the same divine light.

Arguments like these forced the Cappadocians to look more deeply into the relationship of the Father, Son, and Holy Spirit than previous writers had. This exploration would lead to subsequent discussions about whether the Holy Spirit proceeds from the Father, or from the Father and the Son (more about this later). Basil of Caesarea wrote *Against Eunomius*, a rationalist who saw the Holy Spirit as an impersonal force (shades of *Star Wars* and "The Force be with you!"), and against the cult-like Pneumatomachi who taught that the Holy Spirit was a creature who served God but was not fully God. Against false teachers like these the Cappodocians maintained that the Holy Spirit is fully divine and is consubstantial (of the same substance) with the Father and the Son. Because of the particular problems they faced, these eastern church pastor-theologians tended to stress both the independence of the three persons of the Trinity, as well as their unity in the Godhead. One of the ways that they stressed the divine unity of the Trinity was to emphasize that the Son and the Holy Spirit derived from God the Father. This means that the relationship between the three persons of the Trinity is grounded in what the three persons *are*, and not in what they *do*. This insight is firmly rooted in the Gospels. In John's "Upper Room Discourses" in Chapter 14, for example, Jesus told his disciples that he was "going away" and twice he promised the disciples that the Father would send the Holy Spirit to them: "another Advocate, to be with you forever. This is the Spirit of truth, whom the world cannot receive, because it neither sees him nor knows him. You know him, because he abides with you, and he will be in you" (John 14:16-17). And again: "The Advocate, the Holy Spirit, whom the Father will send in my name, will teach you everything, and remind you of all that I have said to you" (John 14:26).

The interrelationship of the Father, Son, and Holy Spirit came to be described by the Greek word *Perichoresis*. It means, literally, "mutual interpretation." It is used to describe the unique way that the Father, Son, and Holy Spirit share in each other's life, nature, ideas, and work. Yet it does not undercut the individuality of the Father, Son, and Holy Spirit. Theologians, especially those of the Greek-speaking church like John of Damascus (ca. 674–749), used *Perichoresis* to describe a "community of being." It means that the Father, Son, and Holy Spirit share in each other's thoughts, will, goals, aspirations, etc., and work together to accomplish these things for us and with us in our human lives. It is like saying, because the Father, Son, and Holy Spirit share the same divine nature

(Godhead), they share the same mind—although each person is free to act and to express themselves in their own distinctive manner.

A second important concept that emerged in these discussions was called "appropriation." This line of thought began in response to the modalists (whom we met in Chapter 2), reached fuller development with the Cappodocians, and received its classic emphasis with Augustine of Hippo (354–430). *Appropriation* was a way of saying that each person of the Trinity was involved in the various works performed by the other members of the Trinity. In Creation, for example, the Father speaks creation into existence by the vehicle of the Word, while the Holy Spirit "swept" over the face of the waters (Genesis 1:2). While it is possible to delineate the particular activities of the respective persons of the Trinity, at basis each work was the work of the same God. In a similar way, the Father sends his Son into the world for our salvation (John 3:16), the Son gives himself as a "ransom" for our sins (Mark 10:45), and the Son goes to the Father to send the Holy Spirit into the lives of believers to "be with you forever" and to "remind you of all that I have said to you" (John 14:16, 26). Hence, it is possible to distinguish the particular works of the Father, Son, and Holy Spirit in matters like Creation, or redemption; but at basis these particular works are all the work of the one God. The Father, Son, and Holy Spirit worked our creation and salvation as a shared work. They "appropriated" or participated in each other's efforts, so that it is possible to say, with Paul, that "in Christ God was reconciling the world to himself" (2 Corinthians 5:19).

> Read John 14. How does the Scripture inform your understanding of *Perichoresis* (community of being of the Trinity) and *appropriation* (involvement of various works of the members of the Trinity)? What contemporary illustrations might be used to describe these ways of thinking about the Trinity?

The Council of Constantinople, in 381, added a section of theological reflection on the Holy Spirit to the Nicene Creed, which has been accepted as part of the Nicene Creed ever since. This addition was almost certainly due to the efforts of the Cappadocians.

Closing

Stand, form a circle, and join hands. Sing stanza 1 of the hymn "Holy, Holy, Holy." Read the following Charles Wesley hymn in unison as a closing prayer.

1. The Lord our God is only One,
   One is Jehovah the most high:
   Jehovah is his name alone,
   Who made and fills both
   earth and sky;
   Jehovah is the Saviour's name;
   Jehovah is the Spirit's too:
   And Three essentially the same
   Is the eternal God and true.

2. The name peculiarly Divine
   Which doth his nature best
   express,
   To the Three Persons we assign,
   And Each Substantial God
   confess;
   Rivals of his celestial host
   We triumph here like those above,
   And Father, Son, and Holy Ghost.
   The One Supreme Jehovah love.[5]

Notes

1. Charles Wesley, *Hymns on the Trinity*, page 5 This hymn is based on Revelation 22:13. It could be used as a responsive reading or sung to a familiar tune like "Carol," used with the hymn "It Came Upon a Midnight Clear," or "Cleansing Fountain," used with the hymn "There Is a Fountain Filled With Blood."

2. Henry Bettenson, ed. *Documents of the Christian Church* (New York: Oxford University Press, 1963), page 39.

3. Bettenson, *Documents*, page 34.

4. Robert Payne, "A Hammer Struck at Heresy," *Christian History*, Volume XV (Summer 1996), Number 3, page 15.

5. Charles Wesley, *Hymns on the Trinity*, page 72. This hymn is based on Deuteronomy 6:4; Psalm 133:18; Jeremiah 32:6; and Ezekiel 8:1, 3. It could be sung to tunes like "Candler," used with the hymn "Come, O Thou Traveler Unknown"; "Jerusalem," used with the hymn "O Day of Peace That Dimly Shines"; or "Sweet Hour," used with the hymn "Sweet Hour of Prayer."

CHAPTER 5
FRESH STARTS OR FALSE STARTS?

Focus: This chapter explores ancient Trinitarian theology after the Council of Nicea.

Gathering

Read or sing the hymn below. You may also read the hymn as a responsive reading.

1. Spirit of truth, essential God,
    Who didst thine ancient
        saints inspire,
    Shed in their hearts thy love
        abroad,
    And touch their hallow'd lips
        with fire,
    Our God from all eternity,
    World without end, we
        worship thee.

2. Still we believe, Almighty Lord,
    Whose presence fills both earth
        and heaven,
    The meaning of the written word
    Is still by inspiration given,
    Thou only dost thyself explain
    The secret mind of God to man.

3. Come, then, Divine Interpreter,
    The Scriptures to our hearts apply,
    And taught by thee we God revere,
    Him in Three Persons magnify,
    In each the Triune God adore,
    Who was, and is for evermore.[1]

Reflect upon the hymn's assertion that the Scriptures witness to the Triune God. What examples come to mind?

One would think that the Council of Nicea and the Nicene Creed would have been sufficient steps to settle the Arian controversy about the doctrine of the Trinity, but that was certainly not the case. Even governmental support, in the person of Emperor Constantine did not thwart the growth of Arianism. Imagining that Arianism would be easily defeated by council or decision would be as naive as assuming that racial prejudice was immediately rooted out by civil rights legislation passed in the 1960's. Victory is sometimes won one-person-at-a-time; so it was with ancient Arianism.

Conflict between Arian and orthodox pastor-theologians continued to rage throughout the fourth century, and Athanasius seemed to have been a lightning rod for controversy; if controversy was going to strike, it seemed certain that it would strike him. He was deposed from church office and exiled no fewer than five times because of the changing currents of Christian theology and church leadership in the fourth century. In fact, if one were looking for a barometer to determine whether Arianism or Christian orthodoxy dominated at any particular time during the next quarter of the fourth century, all a person needed to do was ask: "Is Athanasius in exile?"

The Nicene Aftermath

Athanasius returned to Alexandria after the Council of Nicea and was soon installed as bishop, succeeding Alexander. He struggled against a policy of rapid readmission of unrepentant Arians and the Meletians (who were heretical with respect to the doctrine of the Holy Spirit). Athanasius extended the episcopal authority of Alexandria as far as the Sudan and Libya, hoping to gradually stamp out Arianism in North Africa. For these efforts he was deposed in 335 for abuse of authority and exiled to Trier (in Germany), which was then the capital of the Roman province of Gaul. This began a lengthy period of "on-again-off-again" episcopates for Athanasius.

Imperial support for ecclesiastical decisions also meant that the Roman emperors felt free to intervene in church affairs, almost at will. When Constantine died in 337, imperial support turned into imperial harassment for Athanasius. Constantine was succeeded by his three sons, two of whom were Arians. When the third of these died, in 361, he was succeeded by the pagan Julian "the apostate," who persecuted and exiled Athanasius not because he was anti-Arian but because he was an effective

Christian bishop; Athanasius was able to return in 363. The Arian emperor, Valens, deposed and exiled Athanasius for the last time in the winter of 365–66. He was eventually recalled, however, because of the popular furor caused by Valens's action against him. Athanasius was rein-stalled as bishop of Alexandria on February 1, 366, and he adorned that office with faithful service until his death on May 2, 373. Athanasius

> Read the Athanasian Creed in Appendix B. What insights do you gain about God, Jesus, and the Holy Spirit from your reading?

was memorialized by a creed that bears his name and faithfully commu-nicates his teaching (*see* Appendix B). While it is not certain whether he actually penned the "Athanasian Creed," it certainly is clear that it reflects the Trinitarian teaching that he proclaimed and taught for more than fifty-five years. And while Athanasius did not live to see his complete vindica-tion and the utter defeat of Arianism, it was not long in coming. In 381, the orthodox Christian emperor, Theodosius, opened the first Council of Constantinople by asking the fathers gathered there to reaffirm the Nicene Creed as a true and faithful summary of Christian teaching that must stand for all time.

Christological Controversies and the Council of Chalcedon

One of the "false starts" of the post-Nicene fourth century was engen-dered by Apollinarius (ca. 310–390), bishop of Laodicea. He had been a good friend of Athanasius and a staunch opponent to the Arians. But when he reached his sixties Apollinarius began teaching a distinctive under-standing of the nature of Christ that was eventually condemned as a heresy at the Council of Constantinople in 381. Apollinarius drew upon classical philosophy, as many Christians did, to explain the composite nature of humans as being comprised of three parts: body, soul, and spirit. In an attempt to emphasize the full divin-

> Look up *Apollinarius* and *Apollinarianism* in a dictionary of church history, on the Internet, or in some other easily accessible resource. How does your research inform your understanding of the debates about the humanity and divinity of Jesus Christ? What does it say to you about Jesus? about the doctrine of the Trinity?

ity of Jesus Christ, Apollinarius posited the notion that Jesus' true human-ity, while being composed of three parts (body, soul, and spirit), had a human body and a human soul; but instead of a human spirit Jesus had the *Logos* or Word of God (John 1:1). While stressing Jesus' uniqueness in a creative way, Apollinarius turned Jesus' "full humanity" into something like two-thirds of full humanity—since no other human could claim to have the *Logos* of God instead of a human spirit. When Apollinarius could not be convinced of his error, his views were condemned by the church.

Almost in reaction to the views of Apollinarius, a scholarly monk named Nestorius (ca. 381–452) developed an understanding of Jesus' dual natures (God and human) in a way that stressed Jesus' humanity—but at the expense of his true divinity. Phraseology and titles ascribing honor to Mary, the mother of Jesus, were beginning to become common in the church at this time. Some people were begin-ning to call Mary *theotokos* or "the God-bearer." Nestorius found this way of speaking dis-tasteful and suggested instead that one should instead say Mary was *Christotokos* or "Christ-bearer," since she was mother of only the human nature of Jesus. The way that Nestorius developed his argu-ments, however, made it clear

> Look up *Nestorius* and *Nestorianism* in a dictionary of church history, on the Internet, or in some other easily acces-sible resource. How does your research inform your understanding of the debates about the humanity and divinity of Jesus Christ? What does it say to you about Jesus? about the doc-trine of the Trinity?

that he viewed the dual natures of Jesus Christ as being stacked one against each other in a rather artificial manner, like flavors of Neopolitan ice cream, rather than joined and integrated into an indissoluble, organic union. His explanations made it seem as though Christ were a moral man, who was—by his morality—joined to the divine. In fact, Nestorius called Jesus "the God-bearer" rather than "the God-Man." This was more equivocation than the church was willing to accept so soon after the Arian controversy. The Nestorians eventually split from the Catholic Church and moved east into Asia establishing churches as far east as China.

A third reaction to these "false starts" on the dual nature of Jesus Christ was engineered by Eutyches (ca. 378–454), a monk who lived and studied in a monastery in Constantinople. In reaction to Nestorianism, which he rightly believed cheapened the true divinity of Jesus Christ, Eutyches developed a theory of the dual natures of Jesus that stressed the predomi-

> Look up *Eutyches* in a dictionary of church history, on the Internet, or in some other easily accessible resource. How does your research inform your understanding of the debates about the humanity and divinity of Jesus Christ? What does it say to you about the doctrine of the Trinity?

nance of the divine over the human. His explanation of the association of the two natures indicates that Eutyches felt that Jesus' divine nature so dominated his human nature that the human nature was fused to the divine nature or absorbed by it. This was also not an acceptable solution, since it essentially destroyed the true humanity of Jesus Christ. Eutyches's views were soundly condemned from various quarters of the church, including the bishop of Rome (or Pope) Leo I—who published a *Tome* against it.

The description of the dual natures of Jesus Christ proved to be a difficult matter for early Christians. It seemed that most theories that were being developed erred either by stressing Jesus' humanity at the expense of his divinity, or by stressing Jesus' divinity at the expense of his humanity. The church met at the Council of Chalcedon in A.D. 456 to develop a "formula" or creedal statement that testified to and affirmed the dual natures of Jesus Christ without falling into the kind of errors developed in earlier explanations. (*See* Appendix C for the "Symbol of Chalcedon.") The views of Nestorius and Eutyches were specifically condemned by the Council of Chalcedon.

> Look up *Council of Chalcedon* in a dictionary of church history, on the Internet, or in some other easily accessible resource. How does your research inform your understanding of the debates about the humanity and divinity of Jesus Christ? What does it say to you about the doctrine of the Trinity? Read "The Symbol (or Creed) of Chalcedon," in Appendix C. How does it address the positions of Apollinarius, Nestorius, and Eutyches?

The Filioque Clause

As the fourth-century Cappodocian fathers turned their attention to "the forgotten member of the Trinity," the Holy Spirit, important matters regarding the full divinity of the third person of the Trinity were explored. One of these matters pertained to "the sending" or "proceeding" of the

Holy Spirit. Jesus said, "I will ask the Father, and he will give you another Advocate ... the Spirit of truth" (John 14:16-17). "If I do not go away, the Advocate will not come to you; but if I go, I will send him to you" (John 16:7). The filioque clause refers to the words "and the Son" that were added to the Nicene Creed in A.D. 589.

> Read John 14:16-17 and 16:7. What do these Scriptures say to you about the Holy Spirit? What do they say to you about the doctrine of the Trinity?

The Nicene Creed, as it was affirmed and ratified by the Council of Constantinople (381), stated that the Holy Spirit "proceedeth from the Father." It was based on Scripture texts, like John 14:16-17, in which Jesus told his disciples that he would pray to the Father and *the Father* would send the Holy Spirit ("the Advocate") upon them. When the Nicene Creed was affirmed at the ecumenical Council of Toledo (in 589), the words "and the Son" were added to the Nicene statement about the coming of the Holy Spirit. The Eastern, Greek-speaking wing of the Christian church refused to accept this addition to the words of the Nicene Creed, and it was more than a matter of pride or nostalgia. Their not wanting the earlier version changed was based in a genuine difference in how the Eastern (Greek-speaking) and Western

> Look up *filioque* in a dictionary of church history, on the Internet, or in some other easily accessible resource. How does your research inform your understanding of the Holy Spirit? What does it say to you about the doctrine of the Trinity?

(Latin-speaking) wings of the ancient church approached the doctrine of the Trinity.

While both the Eastern and Western churches affirmed that the Holy Spirit was truly divine and a full-fledged person of the Trinity, co-equal, co-eternal, and consubstantial with the Father and the Son, it seemed that the Greek fathers thought of the divine relationships within the Trinity differently from the Western fathers. Beginning with the Cappodocian fathers, the Eastern church had stressed the diversity of persons within the Trinity and worked from the plurality, *persons,* toward the *unity* of the divine being and essence; they started with the "three-ness" of the Trinity and expressed the "oneness" of the Godhead within that context. One of the main ways that the Greek fathers stressed the "oneness" of the

Godhead was to point out that the Father alone was the sole source of the Godhead; both the Son and the Holy Spirit drew their existence and their divinity from the Father. The Son and the Holy Spirit are said to come out of the Father in similar but different ways. As we noted, with respect to the Arian question, the Son is "begotten" (John 1:18) out of the Father, whereas the Holy Spirit "proceedeth" from the Father (John 15:26).

By stressing that the Son and the Holy Spirit both come out of the Father, the Eastern fathers felt that they had a very biblical and concrete way of showing how the three persons of the Trinity really are the same divine substance. It was also grounded in their appreciation for the scriptural metaphors used for describing Son as "the Word of God" (John 1:1), whereas the Holy Spirit is "the breath of God" (from the New Testament Greek word *spirit*, which can be translated "wind" or "breath"). The Cappodocian fathers were fond of saying that God the Father spoke creation into existence by pronouncing his Word, but as God spoke God also breathed out the Holy Spirit so that the Word might be effective among us. This becomes a model for explaining how God works in the world. The Father pronounces his Word and at the same time breathes out the Holy Spirit so that the Word can be heard and received. This was an argument about more than semantics. It had to do with the way the Greek fathers preferred to explain the oneness of God, and indeed, to explain how God works in the world.

The Latin-speaking, Western church, following the lead of St. Augustine and others, argued that the Holy Spirit had to be thought of as proceeding from both the Father and the Son. One of his proof texts for this point of view was John 20:22, where the risen Christ breathed on his disciples and told them, "Receive the Holy Spirit." But it was rooted in the deeper distinction caused by the fact that the Western church tended to begin her discussions of the Trinity by starting with the oneness of the Godhead and explaining the plurality of persons within the Godhead by describing the equality of work and relationships within the Trinity. The equality of relationships the Latin fathers cherished within the Trinity

> Create a sketch or diagram that illustrates views of the Holy Spirit in relation to God the Father and the Son in both the Eastern and the Western traditions. What difference does the filioque clause, "and the Son," make in the sketch?

68

seemed upset by the Greek fathers' insistence that the Son and the Holy Spirit come out from the Father. This disagreement over the "procession of the Holy Spirit" remained an unresolved source of irritation between the Greek and Latin churches and contributed, no doubt, to their formal split in A.D.1054.

Augustine's Fresh Start

Augustine (354–430) was Bishop of Hippo in North Africa. He was a brilliant theologian, philosopher, and church leader who gave the doctrine of the Trinity careful consideration in his book *On the Trinity*. The nature of God was one of the questions that haunted Augustine, even in his pre-conversion years. When he became a Christian he devoted years of prayerful reflection to the topic and began writing *On the Trinity* in 399; the work was not completed till 419, and it is often considered to be his greatest theological work. Drawing upon and improving previous works and concepts, Augustine's *On the Trinity* was the most complete and elaborate discussion that had been devoted to the topic.

> Look up *Augustine* in a dictionary of church history, on the Internet, or in some other easily accessible resource. Talk about the results of your research during the group session. If possible, obtain a copy of his book *On The Trinity* to use as a resource in the group.

Augustine did not attempt to "prove" the doctrine of the Trinity; instead he hoped to defend it from attack and to explain it to Christians and to those inquiring about the faith. He accepted the doctrine of the Trinity simply based upon the biblical revelation. In the first four books (or chapters) of his work Augustine surveyed in great detail the scriptural information in support of the Trinity; in his view, the doctrine of the Trinity is proclaimed on nearly every page of the Bible.

His starting point, with respect to the presentation of his own view of the Trinity, was with the unity of God and unity of the divine "essence" (or substance). This distinguished Augustine's work from that of the Cappodocians and other theologians of the Eastern church, who tended to start with the three persons of the Trinity and then stress their unity by the unique and parallel descent of the Son and the Holy Spirit from God the Father. Augustine's approach to explaining the Trinity, in beginning with the oneness of the Godhead and the unity of divine essence, would mark out the path that Western Christianity would follow ever after with respect to the doctrine of the Trinity. Because of the shared divine essence, each of the three persons of the Trinity cooperate with each other in divine tasks like Creation, Incarnation, the death of Christ, the Resurrection, and the calling of persons to faith. While Father, Son, and Holy Spirit take distinctive expression and have distinct works, they all share equally in the Godhead and for that reason are able to "appropriate" the will, thoughts, and works of the other two divine persons.

With respect to the procession of the Holy Spirit, Augustine established the Western pattern of affirming that the Holy Spirit proceeded both from the Father and the Son; this view, he believed, was demanded by the biblical texts and fit well the symmetry of shared essence and shared works that he stressed in his approach to the doctrine of the Trinity. He was completely in support of what would become the "filioque clause" ("and the Son") and fixed Western church tradition solidly upon that point of view. Augustine says, "... in that supreme trinity which God is there are no intervals of time by which it could be shown, or even asked, whether the Son was first born from the Father, and afterward the Holy Spirit proceeded from them both, seeing that the holy scripture calls him the Spirit of them both.... And many other texts of the divine utterances can be brought in evidence to prove that the one who is properly called in the

> What is your response to Augustine's view of the Holy Spirit in relation to the Father and the Son?

trinity the Holy Spirit is the Spirit of the Father and the Son; the Son himself says of him, *whom I shall send you from the Father* (Jn 15:26), and in another place, *whom the Father will send in my name* (Jn 14:26). He is proved to proceed from each of them, because the Son himself says, *he proceeds from the Father* (Jn 15:26); and then after rising from the dead and appearing to the disciples, *he breathed on them and said, Receive the Holy Spirit* (Jn 20:22) in order to show that the Spirit too is the virtue which went out of him, as we read in the gospel, and healed them all."[2]

Augustine's most original contribution to explaining the Trinity may have been his willingness to use analogies to help his readers enter into his thinking about the doctrine. While he recognized the limitations of these analogies, he also believed that they helped humans conceptualize the Trinity in useful ways. For example, beginning with the assertion that "God is love" (1 John 4:8)—this is a way of speaking of the divine essence—and yet it takes three forms of expression: the lover, the object loved, and the love which unites them. "A trinity is certainly what we are looking for, and not any kind of trinity either but the one that God is, the true and supreme and only God.... Here you are then—when I who am engaged on this search love something, there are three: I myself, what I love, and love itself. For I do not love love unless I love it loving something, because there is no love where nothing is being loved. So then there are three, the lover, and what is being loved, and love."[3]

> How does the assertion "God is love" help you understand the Trinity?

In a similar way, Augustine found a trinity at work in the human mind or psyche. The essence of the matter is knowledge and it takes expression as the mind (that is, our knowledge of ourselves), then in our understanding (the function of our will or love, which sets self-knowledge in motion), and finally in our remembering, knowing, and loving God who is the source of this triune nature in humans who are created in God's own image (Genesis 1:26). He says, "But with these three, when mind knows and loves itself the trinity remains of mind, love, knowledge. Nor are they jumbled up together in any kind of mixture, though they are each one in itself and each whole in their total, whether each in the other two or the other two in each, in any case all in all."[4]

We continue to use analogies as mental "object lessons" for the doctrine of the Trinity, yet it is also important to recognize their shortcomings. One of my favorites is the example of water, which is the same chemical substance whether it takes the form of a liquid, a solid (as ice), or a gas (as steam). But the analogy to the Trinity also breaks down when we recognize that water cannot appear in all three separate forms at the same time, whereas the Trinity can and frequently does do so. Another analogy we sometimes use is that of the egg: we have three parts: the yoke, shell, and white all comprise the whole egg. Yet is it difficult

> What examples best illustrate the Trinity for you?

to think of these as three equal parts, especially when we are making an omelet—I'll take mine without any shell, if you please! A third common analogy for the Trinity is found in the nature of a person and her roles: the same woman can be a wife, mother, and daughter at the same time. But once again, the analogy breaks down as these three "persons" are more functions of the same woman than like the distinct divine persons of the Trinity.

71

The Middle Ages

The medieval period of church history is somewhat like an epilogue to Augustine's approach to the doctrine of the Trinity. Two important developments occurred, but both developments stand on the shoulders of the complete domination of Augustine's theology of the Trinity in the Western church. The first was engendered by the work of Anselm of Canterbury (ca. 1033–1109) who linked Trinitarian reflection to the theology of salvation with a passion that would have pleased Athanasius quite well. Drawing upon the language of metaphors of chivalry to address the intellectuals of the age, Anselm seemed to liken God the Father to the lord of the manor, to whom fealty was owed. Humans violate the obligation of honor when they sin, and thereby dishonor God. Since this is a debt owed by all humans, it is so huge that no human could pay it. Yet, because this debt is owed by humans, a man needs to pay it. Hence, the Father sends forth his champion, the Son of God incarnate, who is a proper mediator between God and humans. As a man, the Word can properly stand as a substitute for all humanity; and as God his life is so valuable it can pay the debt that no human could pay. It is as the God-Man that Jesus Christ, eternal Word of God incarnate, wins our redemption from sin and death.

The second development comes to us from Thomas Aquinas (1125–74). Thomas's approach to the Trinity was drawn directly from Augustine's *On the Trinity* (principally books 1–8), but it was set in the standard question-and-answer form of the day in Aquinas's *Summa Theologica.*

> Look up *Thomas Aquinas* and *Summa Theologica* in a dictionary of church history, on the Internet, or in some other easily accessible resource. Talk about the results of your research in the group. How does your research inform your view of the Trinity?

Thomas's massive *Summa Theologica* was begun in 1256; and he had not completed the work, despite his daily efforts, when he died nearly twenty years later. The work is more like a theological encyclopedia than anything that had preceded it, and it set the doctrine of the Trinity in a form (an Augustinian form) that it would retain for many centuries. Indeed, when the sixteenth-century Catholic Reformation met at the Council of Trent (ca. 1565), it declared that Thomas Aquinas would be viewed as the "standard theologian" of the church. This gave Thomas's (and really Augustine's) construal of the Trinity a preferred status among Roman Catholics that it retained right down to Vatican II (1962). While the Roman Catholic Church rallied around the theology of Thomas Aquinas, the doctrine of the Trinity continued to undergo further development and exploration by Protestant pastors and theologians.

Closing

Stand, form a circle, and join hands. Sing stanza 1 of the hymn "Holy, Holy, Holy." Read the following Charles Wesley hymn in unison as a closing prayer.

1. Whene'er our day of Pentecost
   Is full come, we surely know
   The Father, Son, and Holy Ghost
   Our God, is manifest below:
   The Son doth in the Father dwell,
   The Father in his Son imparts
   His Spirit of joy unspeakable,
   And lives for ever in our hearts.

2. Our hearts are then convinc'd indeed.
   That Christ is with the Father one;
   The Spirit that doth from Both proceed.
   Attests the Co-eternal Son;
   The Spirit of truth and holines
   Asserts his own Divinity:
   And then the Orthodox confess
   One glorious God in Persons Three.[5]

Notes

1. Charles Wesley, *Hymns on the Trinity*, pages 42–43. This hymn is based on 2 Timothy 3:16 and 2 Peter 1:21. It may be sung to "Careys," used with the hymn "Lord God, Your Love Has Called Us Here," or "St. Catherine," used with the hymn "Faith of Our Fathers."

2. Edmund Hill, trans. *Saint Augustine: The Trinity* (Brooklyn: New City Books, 2000), V, pages 430–31. All citations are from this edition.

3. *The Trinity*, IX, 1, pages 270–72.

4. *The Trinity*, IX, page 275.

5. Charles Wesley, *Hymns on the Trinity*, page 42. This hymn was written as a reflection upon John 14:20. It may be sung as a closing hymn to tunes like "Candler," used with the hymn "Come, O Thou Traveler Unknown"; "Jerusalem," used with the hymn "O Day of Peace That Dimly Shines"; or "Sweet Hour," used with the hymn "Sweet Hour of Prayer."

CHAPTER 6
WHAT ARE THEY SAYING ABOUT THE TRINITY?

Focus: This chapter explores modern and contemporary approaches to the Trinity.

Gathering

Read or sing the hymn below. You may also read the hymn as a responsive reading.

1. Triumph, happy soul, to whom
    God the heavenly secret tells
 Father, Son, and Spirit come,
    One in Three Himself reveals!
 What from man thou could'st
    not know,
    Thou art truly taught of God,
 When He doth the faith bestow,
    Wash thee in thy Saviour's
    blood.

2. Fully certified thou art
    By that sacred blood applied,
 He who dwells within thy heart,
    God, the great Jehovah died:
 Now, and not' till now thou knowest
    (Mist'ry learnt by faith alone)
 Father, Son, and Holy Ghost,
    God in Persons Three is One.

3. God in Persons Three, appear
   God to every troubled breast,
   Show Thyself the Comforter,
   Be the weary sinner's rest
   Stranger to thy people's peace,
   Burthen'd with our sins we
   groan;
   Come, that all our griefs may
   cease,
   Take possession of thy own.

4. Father, Son, and Holy Ghost,
   Heal thy creature's misery;
   Thee, the Pearl which Adam lost,
   Give us to recover Thee,
   Give us in pure love renew'd
   Higher by our fall to rise,
   Image of the Triune God,
   House of One who fills
   the skies.[1]

This hymn suggests that the Trinity helps humanity find "the Pearl which Adam lost." What reflections about our salvation and renewal does this hymn suggest to you?

While Protestant reformers like Martin Luther (1483–1546) and John Calvin (1509–64) made intentional departures from Roman Catholic conceptions of the church, sacraments, and the various aspects of popular piety (relics, pilgrimages, and so on), they did not completely reject the theological inheritance that they received through the Roman Catholic tradition. Among the "received tradition" that the founders of Lutheranism and Presbyterianism both affirmed and retained, almost without further reflection, was the doctrine of the Trinity; and they affirmed it in the form that Augustine had established nearly ten centuries before. Indeed, for both Protestant patriarchs, Augustine was a kind of long-distance theological mentor.

What would you consider to be a "received tradition" in your local church? If you grew up in church, what were the "received traditions" there? How do these "received traditions" inform your faith?"

Luther and Calvin

That the doctrine of the Trinity was a settled matter, in Martin Luther's mind, is obvious from how little he actually wrote about it. In his view, this was not one of the church's doctrines and practices that needed to be "reformed"; so he went on to more pressing matters. As a pastor, however, he preached the lectionary texts of Scripture; and his sermons from Trinity Sunday have survived. These sermons offer a rather complete, traditional explication of the doctrine. Affirming the Trinity was, for Luther, as basic to Christian faith as affirming the Apostles' Creed; in fact, he believed that the creed taught the doctrine of the Trinity. Luther wrote, "So the Creed confesses three persons as comprehended in one divine essence, each one, however, retaining his distinct personality; and in order that the simple Christian may recognize that there is but one divine essence and one God, who is tri-personal, a special work, peculiar to himself, is ascribed to each person. And such acts, peculiar to each person, are mentioned for the reason that thus a confusion of persons is avoided. To the Father we ascribe the work of creation; to the Son the work of Redemption; to the Holy Spirit the power to forgive sins, to gladden, to strengthen, to transport from death to life eternal."[2] Like Athanasius, Augustine, and Anselm before him, Luther located the importance of the Trinity for us, in connection with the theology of salvation. For this reason, perhaps, he had little patience with idle speculation about the hidden nature of the triune God and was much more concerned that we direct our attention to God as revealed in Jesus Christ. Hence, Luther wrote: "God's actual divine essence and his will, administration and works—are absolutely beyond all human thought, human understanding or wisdom; in short, that they are and ever will be incomprehensible, inscrutable, and altogether hidden to human reason.... If anything is to be ascertained, it must be through revelation alone; that is, the Word of God, which was sent from heaven."[3] Luther's "Christo-centricity," his Christ-centered focus in Christian theology, caused him to look more directly to Jesus Christ and Christ's gift of our salvation than to the theology of the Trinity *per se*.

> What insights do you gain from Luther's sermon quotes about his understanding of the Trinity?

John Calvin also accepted the doctrine of the Trinity as received Christian truth. In his view, God "so proclaims himself the sole God as to offer himself to be contemplated clearly in three persons. Unless we grasp these, only the bare and empty name of God flits about in our brains, to the exclusion of the true God."[4] The Trinity was so deeply woven into Calvin's theology that his *Institutes of the Christian Religion* (1559), which was arguably the single most important book of the Protestant Reformation, was structured around the concept: Book One focuses our attention upon God the Creator (Father), Book Two upon Jesus Christ our redeemer, and Book Three upon the Holy Spirit who works justification and sanctification in our lives. After dispensing with the Trinity, he went on in Book Four to treat the church and sacraments. While Calvin offered more extended discussion of the aspects of the Trinity (person, substance, and so on) than Luther did, it is also clear that Calvin's chief interest in the Trinity is read through the lens of Christian salvation.

> What connections do you make between the Trinity and salvation?

John and Charles Wesley

John (1703–91) and Charles Wesley (1707–88), co-founders of the Methodist movement, wrote their sermons and hymns at a time when the fashionable and intellectual elite of England were turning toward Deism. Deism was a rational, anti-supernaturalist version of Christianity that sought to square religion with the discoveries of modern philosophy and science by jettisoning miraculous events from the Christian story, as well as other supernatural elements like the unique divinity of Jesus Christ and his resurrection. The God of Deism was like a great watchmaker, who had constructed an orderly universe that runs by natural law and then stood back to observe (but not interfere with) its operations. The rational reduction of Christianity by Deism gave rise to a practical Unitarianism by stripping Jesus of unique divinity and by ignoring discourse about the Holy Spirit. God was so distant and uninvolved in human life that, apart, from God's roles as initial Creator and final Judge who repays humans according to their deeds at the end of time, God plays a very small role in the system. It is a human-centered, ethical, good-works-centered philosophy. The doctrine of the Trinity was under tacit attack from Deism and from the emergence of English Unitarianism (which the Wesleys termed "Arianism").

John Wesley's most concerted explication of the Trinity is found in his "Standard Sermon" number 55, "On the Trinity"; but the doctrine is treated all across the Wesleyan literary corpus, through sermons, journals, tracts, and letters. Wesley proclaimed the doctrine of the Trinity because he was convinced that it faithfully summarizes what the Bible teaches about God. While he refrained from using words like *fundamental doctrines* or *essential truths*, Wesley considered this to be one of the most important of the Bible's doctrines: "There are some truths more important than others. It seems there are some of which are of deep importance.... But surely there are some which it nearly concerns us to know, as having a close connection with vital religion. And doubtless we may rank among these that contained in the words ...: 'There are three that bear record in heaven, the Father, the Word, and the Holy Ghost: and these three are one.'"[5] While Wesley stressed the absolute importance of the doctrine for "vital" or living Christian faith, he refrained from demanding any particular explication of the doctrine or even the use of the word *Trinity*—in the event someone objected to using a nonbiblical expression—so long as a person embraced the Bible's affirmations about it. To use Wesley's expression: one can readily believe the revealed "fact" of the Trinity, without comprehending its "manner."[6] After mounting a lengthy and spirited defense of the importance of believing in things that are to some degree mysterious, apparently as necessary in the "Age of Reason" as it is today, John Wesley wrapped up his sermon "On the Trinity" by arguing that doctrine is proven inwardly, through the witness of the Holy Spirit within Christians; Wesley doubted that "anyone can be a Christian believer" until he or she has this witness. "I know not how anyone can be a Christian believer till 'he hath' (as St. John speaks) 'the witness in himself'; till 'the Spirit of God witnesses with his spirit that he is a child of God'—that is, in effect, till God the Holy Ghost witnesses that God the Father has accepted him through the merits of God the Son—and having this witness he honours the Son and the blessed Spirit 'even as he honours the Father.'"[7]

Charles Wesley's Trinitarian hymns are employed throughout this work

> Locate a copy of Wesley's sermon, "On the Trinity." Read the entire sermon. What issues, questions, or insights do you gain from your reading? Talk about the sermon in the group.

> Read again the Wesley hymns in the "Gathering" and "Closing" activities of this study book. Jot down questions or insights that you gain from your reading. Talk about these in the group. If you have time, you may want to plan a Trinity hymn sing using the tunes suggested in the endnotes. Organize the hymn sing to include a church dinner.

as devotional aids. In 1767, Charles developed *Hymns on the Trinity*, which followed the outline and Scripture texts offered in a current work by William Jones entitled *The Catholic Doctrine of a Trinity* (1756). After producing 136 hymns from Scripture texts for all four topical headings in Jones's book ("The Divinity of Christ," "The Divinity of the Holy Ghost," "The Plurality of the Trinity of Persons," and "The Trinity in Unity"), Charles went on to offer fifty-two additional "Hymns and Prayers to the Trinity" based on Scripture texts of his own choosing. While this was the most concentrated work on the Trinity that Charles Wesley produced, the doctrine is affirmed and celebrated all across his huge corpus of hymns and sacred poems.

Modern Theology

Friedrich Schleiermacher (1768–1834) is generally considered to be the "father of modern theology" because he set a new pattern for doing theology that held sway among many Protestants in the modern era. Showing the impact of modern philosophy, psychology, and literary criticism of the Bible, Schleiermacher and theologians like him were looking for a new way to approach the task of Protestant theology. Schleiermacher decided that the most appropriate place to begin theologizing was human experience. This meant that Christian doctrines were to be understood as explanations of human experiences, feelings, or religious attitudes. His *The Christian Faith* (1821) was constructed upon the premise that "Christian doctrines are accounts of the Christian religious affections set forth in speech."[8]

The doctrine of the Trinity became a problem for Schleiermacher's approach to theology, however, precisely because of his methodological commitments; his chief difficulty was that the most important matters about the Trinity are really about God's nature, not about human self-consciousness. As he noted: "This doctrine itself, as ecclesiastically framed, is not an immediate utterance concerning the Christian self-con-

> What strengths do you see in beginning thought about God, Jesus, and the Holy Spirit in the realm of "human God-consciousness"? What weaknesses do you see?

sciousness, but only a combination of several such utterances."[9] For this reason, then, Schleiermacher relegated the doctrine of the Trinity to a twenty-page appendix at the end of his *Christian Faith*, in which he attempted to reshape the doctrine from the standpoint of human God-consciousness. In the final analysis, however, he was forced to conclude that the matter must remain unsettled. "We have the less reason to regard this doctrine as finally settled since it did not receive any fresh treatment when the Evangelical (Protestant) Church was set up; and so there must still be in store for it a transformation which will go back to its very beginnings."[10]

Two important theological trajectories emerged from Schleiermacher's work. The first was his methodology. Many modern theologians who followed after him became willing to start with "Christian self-consciousness"—this signaled a major shift in the way theology would be "done." Previous theologians had started with God, God's revelation, and Scripture, which has been called "theology from above" because of the mental picture of it coming down from heaven. After Schleiermacher, Protestant theologians were willing to begin with human experience, and this signaled a shift toward "theology from below" with its starting point in human life rather than in the life of God. The second bequest that came to modern theology from Schleiermacher was the simple fact that the Trinity was no longer considered a "settled" doctrine. This opened the door to many fresh, new, and creative inquiries into the doctrine of the Trinity.

Karl Barth

It is difficult to imagine a modern theologian whose work was more antithetical to the work of Friedrich Schleiermacher than was that of Karl Barth (1886–1968). Unlike Schleiermacher, who saved the Trinity for the end of his theological tome, Barth came to the subject early, in chapter two of his first volume. Barth could not think of starting his theological inquiry anywhere but Holy Scripture, and in his view even a casual reading of the Bible suggested that it is about God and not about human religious consciousness. He noted, for example, "When Holy Scripture speaks of God it concentrates our attention and thoughts upon one single point and what is to be known at that point. And what is to be known there is quite simple. It is the God who in the first person singular addressed the patriarchs and Moses, the prophets and later the apostles. It is the God who in this 'I' is and has and reveals sovereignty and all other perfections."[11] Barth was equally clear as to what this "one single point" of divine revelation amounts to: "If in this way we ask further concerning the one point upon which, according to Scripture, our attention and thoughts should and must be concentrated, then from first to last the Bible directs us to the name of Jesus Christ. It is in this name that we discern the divine decision in favour of the movement towards this people, the self-determination of God as Lord and Shepherd of this people and the determination of this people as 'his people, and the sheep of his pasture' (Ps. 100)."[12]

In the Trinity we are not dealing with three separate divine egos, but three modes of one divine "I." For Barth, the Trinity was "received Christian doctrine," it was a closed issue: "The language of the early Church states that God is three persons. In the way in which the early Church understood the concept of person, this concept is unassailable."[13] Barth was comfortable with the Trinitarian language of Scripture and the ancient church, properly understood. By following the Protestant reformers in their Christo-centric focus within the Trinity, Barth also joined Luther and Calvin in persistently viewing the Trinity through the lens of our salvation: "The One God is by nature and in eternity the Father, the source of His Son and, in union with Him, the source of the Holy Spirit. In virtue of this way of being of His He is by grace the Father of all men, whom He calls in time, in His Son and through His Spirit, to be His children."[14]

> What strengths do you see in Barth's method of looking to "received tradition" for his views about God, Jesus, and the Holy Spirit? What weaknesses? How do Barth's quotations speak to you about the Trinity?

Liberation Theology

Most contemporary theologies of the Trinity begin with specific aspects of human experience. Liberation theology is one of the most influential of these contemporary theologies, and it takes its starting point with the fact and experience of human oppression—largely in a Latin American context. This oppression is viewed as being full-orbed. It is physical, political, economic, and because it is a composite of all of these, it is also an oppression of the human spirit. Leonardo Boff (b. 1938), is a Franciscan priest and professor of theology at The Franciscan Institute in Petropolis, Brazil. Boff persistently turns his attention to the role of the Trinity in the process of human liberation. His *Trinity and Society* (1988) is his most sustained examination of the topic.

The core concept of *Trinity and Society* is the doctrine of *perichoresis*—the intimate, inter-Trinitarian communion that exists between the Father, Son, and Holy Spirit. Boff views the holy community that exists within the Godhead as the most appropriate model for human community. Since the inter-Trinitarian community is one of equality and mutual love, it offers significant promise as a liberating and justice-producing communion with God. He

> What thoughts and/or feelings come to you when you hear the word *liberation*? What connections do you see between salvation and liberation? What biblical stories come to mind?

feels that the monarchical or dominion model, which depicts God as a great Sovereign on his throne, has been employed in ways that have been unnecessarily exploitative or oppressive. The communal dimension of the Trinity holds more promise as a resolution to the problems faced by contemporary Christians, particularly contemporary Christians living in Latin America. It moderates the extreme disparities that capitalism has created between the "haves" and the "have nots" in this hemisphere.

God the Father is the origin of all human liberation in a theological, political, spiritual, and psychological sense. Boff says, "There are many ways of seeing God as Father. In cosmology God is seen as Father for having created the universe: this is a common appellation in world religions. In the *political* sense, in which it is used in the Old Testament, God is Father for having created, chosen and freed his people.... In a *spiritual* sense, God is Father because he shows pity and mercy, because he is the refuge and protection of the pious, the sinners and the abandoned.... In a *psychological* sense, God is experienced as Father as the final consolation in human loneliness, the utopic realization of our thirst for immortality and omnipotence."[15] Boff reminded his readers, however, that "Christian faith has no image of God the Father."[16] This fact places enormous significance upon the role of the Son: "This Father, unfathomable mystery, was revealed to us by Jesus Christ, his only-begotten Son."[17] The second person of the Trinity, not only reveals the Father, but is, as Boff describes him, the "Mediator of Integral Liberation."[18] Boff says, "As long as the incarnate Word has not set all creation free through the cross, God still cannot be 'all in all' (1Cor. 15:28). The lordship of the incarnate, crucified and risen Word consists in the immense process of liberation from the sin that hides the glory of the Father. So, as the Word goes on bringing in the

Kingdom of life, liberty, reconciliation, and peace, he redeems the sonship of all created beings, particularly of human beings in the position of captivity in which they now find themselves. Only through that redemption will we see the triumph of the Kingdom of the Trinity, of the Father, Son, and Holy Spirit, and of creation as part of the communion [*perichoresis*] of the Trinity."[19] In a similar way, he describes the Holy Spirit as the "Driving Force of Integral Liberation."[20] In this sense, then, the Holy Spirit is "the father of the poor (*pater pauperum*), giving them strength to resist, courage to rise up, creativity to find new ways. In order to build up a world founded on truth, justice, and love, the social order must be changed on a deep level, and 'God's Spirit ... is not absent from this development.'"[21]

Christian Feminism

Christian feminists have critiqued traditional conceptualizations of God and the terminology used to express the doctrine of the Trinity. Beginning with the life situation of Christian women, feminists point out that the church has participated in patriarchal patterns of organization and leadership and hence given credence to social standards and practices that have been restrictive and oppressive toward women. The church has not always lived up to the Pauline injunction: "There is no longer Jew or Greek, there is no longer slave or free, there is no longer male and female; for all of you are one in Christ Jesus" (Galatians 3:28). In fact, in some instances the Christian church has been more willing to exclude women from leadership or full participation in church life in ways that even exceed women's oppression in the larger culture. The participation of the church in the exclusion and oppression of women has caused Christian feminists to operate with a "hermeneutics of suspicion." This means that they are suspicious of traditional religious forms and expressions until it is clear that they do not exploit women or create a climate in which women are treated unfairly. Mary Daly has placed this situation in sharp focus with her slogan: "If

> Read Galatians 3:28. What does the Scripture say to you about the way God values human beings? In what ways might the use of gender language about God, either male or female, cause people to feel excluded? How do you think about God?

God is male, then the male is god."[22] Feminists point out that the traditional Trinitarian language of "Father, Son, and Holy Spirit" seems to imply that two-thirds of the Trinity is male.

Recognizing the power of religious language when it comes to shaping reality, Christian feminists, like Sallie McFague, have looked for new metaphors and new models for expressing the Christian understanding of God in ways that are more hospitable to women and their particular concerns. In her work *Models of God*, McFague dismisses the traditional "monarchical model" of God, which pictures God functioning as a sovereign king, as being outmoded and potentially harmful because of the excessive distance it creates between God and humans. She opts for a more organic, relational model in which the world is seen as God's body and God's triune nature is understood and named by the three New Testament Greek words for love: *agape*, *eros*, and *philia*. In this way she designates the Trinity as Mother, Lover, and Friend.[23] The emphasis upon the world as God's body stresses the immanence or closeness of God and God's involvement in the human situation, in pain, suffering, and ecological issues. The central motif that comes with God as Mother is Creator and along with that comes God as Creator of Justice. She says, "God as lover is the one who loves the world not with the fingertips but totally and passionately, taking pleasure in its variety and richness, finding it attractive and valuable, delighting in its fulfillment. God as lover is the moving power of love in the universe, the desire for unity with all the beloved, the passionate embrace that spins the 'living pulsing earth' around, sends 'the blood through our veins,' and 'draws us into one another's arms.' "[24] Summarizing her exploration of the metaphor God as Friend, Sallie McFague wrote: "As a model of God's relationship with the world, it says that we do not belong to ourselves, but it also says we are not left to ourselves. In stressing mutuality, commitment, trust, common vision, and interdependence, it denies possession but defies despair. It is a model of hope: God is with us, immanent in the world as our friend and co-worker and immanent in the community of friends called the church."[25]

In this reconstruction McFague insists she is not interested in simply replacing God as "Father" with God as "Mother"; rather she is concerned

> What is your response to the assertion that God has many names? What names might you use for each person of the Trinity? What would your name say about the Trinity?

to explore the question whether other models or names of God more adequately fit the needs of the contemporary situation. She writes: "If it can be shown that models other than the traditional ones are appropriate and illuminating for expressing the Christian gospel in our time, an important admission will have been made: *God has many names*. The attempt to unseat both monarchical and traditional trinitarian language, however, is not a subterfuge to establish a new trinity using different names. To do so would be to fall into the 'tyranny of the absolutizing imagination,' which we have all along tried to avoid."[26]

Process Theology

Process theology is characterized by its distinctive "cosmology" (theology of the world and how it works), which is based upon the philosophy of Alfred North Whitehead (1861–1947). Drawing upon developmental themes from philosophy and nuclear science (with respect to the motion of molecules), process theology sees the world as being in a state of constant motion and development; even the solidity that we observe in the world is an illusion, because beneath it is the rapid and sometimes random motion of molecules and atoms. Yet within this motion and development there are moments that are utterly concrete and provide the bases for new developments, new understandings, and new experiences. God is viewed as the creative energy that moves this process forward toward new and creative expressions and experiences.

God is viewed as being bipolar, that is, as having two natures; and through both natures God is deeply involved in the endless processes of the world. God has a "primordial" or transcendent nature, which is expressed in the timeless perfections of God's character, and God has a "consequent" or immanent nature through which God takes part in the world process. Marjorie Hewitt Suchocki (b. 1933) has written an important work, *God, Christ, Church: A Practical Guide to Process Theology*, which views the main Christian doctrines from the perspective of process theology.[27] In *God, Christ, Church*, Suchocki stresses that the process cosmology is primarily a relational model.

Exploring the human condition of loneliness, Suchocki urges the reader to discover the presence of God, which not only is a balm to our loneliness but also draws us back into to relationship with God and with others: "When in our loneliness we touch God, we know ourselves as also touched by God, and in the knowing, we are open to the pervasiveness of the divine presence. But it is the nature of the divine presence to nudge us back to the world, pushing us toward renewed attention to the content of that touching, guiding, creating aim for our good. The aim inexorably directs us toward our best way of constituting ourselves through and for the world."[28] God's wisdom is expressed through the perfect correlation between the wisdom of God's primordial nature and God's consequent (immanent) nature. When the world is a confusing place, it gives us comfort to know that God knows and goes with us into all of life's uncertainties: "The effect of God's wisdom is that no matter what threats and contingencies we may experience, God is faithful to lead us into a creative mode of dealing with these problems. This follows from the fact that God's wisdom is not a cold calculation of bits and pieces of knowledge, as if God were some gigantic computer knowing all things and feeding information to the world. Rather, God's wisdom follows from the divine feeling, wherein God feels the world and thus knows the world in a coexperience."[29] In examining God's power, Suchocki concludes that God's power and the interdependent nature of the cosmos

> What does Suchocki's doctrine of the Trinity say about God? about our own experience of God?

give us profound hope that love and justice will be expressed in the world. She writes: "Given the role of God's power in the achievement of justice, and given our increased awareness of our own responsibilities in an interdependent universe, there is a ground for hope despite injustice.... God influences the world in keeping with the divine character, and thus leads the world toward modes of justice. So we can address the evils of our existence in the hope that they can be overcome."[30] After an extensive examination of the divine attributes of presence, wisdom, and power, Suchocki turned her attention to the doctrine of the Trinity in the "Conclusion" of her work. From this it is clear that she considers the Trinity the integrating concept that best summarizes her work: " 'Trinity' denotes the magnitude of the divine power that accomplishes the vision of the divine wisdom, all within the everlasting unity of presence. Presence, wisdom, and power: those qualities we perceive in our own experience of God for us can be understood in reference to the divine nature itself when that nature is expressed as complexity in unity, trinity. Thus 'trinity' is a symbol that faces in two directions. There is the God-ward signification, in which the symbol expresses our sense of the divine subjectivity, and there is the world-ward direction, in which the symbol speaks of our own experience of God."[31]

Closing

Stand, form a circle, and join hands. Sing stanza 1 of the hymn "Holy, Holy, Holy." Read the following stanzas from Charles Wesley's hymn in unison as a closing prayer.

2. Not from our Creeds alone
    The doctrine we receive:
    Jehovah Three in One,
    He gives us to believe,
    The God of truth Himself imparts,
    And writes his name upon our hearts.

3. His Son on us bestow'd
    The Father hath reveal'd;
    The Son his Father show'd
    From mortal eye conceal'd;
    Th' indwelling Comforter attests
    That One is Three, in faithful breasts.[32]

Notes

1. Charles Wesley, *Hymns on the Trinity*, page 95. Sing it to a tune like "Aberstwyth," used with the hymn "Jesus, Lover of My Soul," or "St. George's Windsor," used with the hymn "Come, Ye Thankful People, Come."

2. Hugh T. Kerr, *A Compend of Luther's Theology* (Philadelphia: Westminster Press, 1974), page 41. All subsequent quotations from Martin Luther will come from this volume.

3. *A Compend of Luther's Theology*, page 39.

4. John McNeill, ed. Ford Lewis Battles, trans., *Calvin: Institutes of the Christian Religion*, 2 volumes (Philadelphia: Westminster Press, 1977); Volume I, page 122. All quotations from Calvin's *Institutes* will come from this edition.

5. Outler, *JW Sermons* II, page 376.

6. Outler, *JW Sermons* II, page 384.

7. Outler, *JW Sermons* II, page 385.

8. H. R. Mackintosh, and J. S. Stewart, eds. Friedrich Schleiermacher, *The Christian Faith* (Edinburgh: T & T Clark, 1948; Harper Torchbooks: Harper & Row, 1963), page 76. All quotations from *The Christian Faith* will come from this edition.

9. *The Christian Faith*, page 738.

10. *The Christian Faith*, page 747.

11. Geoffrey Bromiley, trans. Karl Barth, *Church Dogmatics: A Selection* (New York: Harper and Row, 1961), page 31.

12. *Church Dogmatics*, pages 31–32.

13. Karl Barth, *Dogmatics in Outline* (New York: Harper and Row, 1959), page 42.

14. *Dogmatics in Outline*, page 42.

15. Leonardo Boff, *Trinity and Society* (Maryknoll, New York: Orbis Books, 1988), page 164. All citations of Boff's work will come from this edition.

16. *Trinity and Society*, page 165.

17. *Trinity and Society*, page 165.

18. *Trinity and Society*, page 178.

19. *Trinity and Society*, page 188.

20. *Trinity and Society,* page 189.

21. *Trinity and Society,* page 194.

22. Mary Daly, *Beyond God the Father* (Boston: Beacon Press, 1973), page 19.

23. Sallie McFague, *Models of God: Theology for an Ecological, Nuclear Age* (Philadelphia: Fortress Press, 1987), pages 69–87. All citations from McFague's work will come from this edition

24. *Models of God*, page 130.

25. *Models of God*, page 167.

26. *Models of God*, page 182.

27. Marjorie Hewitt Suchocki, *God, Christ, Church: A Practical Guide to Process Theology* (New York: Crossroad, 1989 revised edition). All citations from *God, Christ, Church* will come from this edition.

28. *God, Christ, Church*, page 61.

29. *God, Christ, Church*, page 70.

30. *God, Christ, Church*, pages 83–84.

31. *God, Christ, Church*, page 229.

32. Charles Wesley, *Hymns on the Trinity*, page 93. The hymn could be sung to tunes like "Lenox," used with the hymn "Blow Ye the Trumpet, Blow," or "Darwall's," used with the hymn "Rejoice, the Lord Is King."

CHAPTER 7
WHAT DOES IT MATTER?

Focus: This chapter explores the relevance of the Trinity for contemporary Christians.

Gathering

Read or sing the hymn below. You may also read the hymn as a responsive reading.

1. Fountain of Divine compassion,
    Father of the ransom'd race,
  Christ, our Saviour and salvation,
    Spirit of consecrating grace;
  See us prostrated before Thee;
    Co-essential Three in One,
  Glorious God, our souls adore Thee
    High on thine eternal throne.

2. While we in thy name assemble,
    Overshadow'd from above,
  Let us at thy presence tremble,
    Holy, Triune God of love;
  Father, Son, and Spirit bless us,
    Who the true Jehovah art:
  Plenitude of God in Jesus,
    Enter every contrite heart.

3. Challenge now thine humble dwelling,
    O Thou High and Lofty One,
  Thy own Deity revealing,
    God in Persons Three come down:
  Thou, the Witnesses in heaven,
    Dost on earth thy record bear:
  Shew us here our sins forgiven,
    Shew us all thy glory there.[1]

How is the Trinity reflected in our lives?

So What?

One of life's important questions, and one that also pertains to theological doctrine, is the question, "So what?" Like Athanasius, Anselm, and commentators of ages gone by, we too need to ask ourselves, "What implications does the doctrine of the Trinity hold for us? What difference does it make to the shape of our Christian lives and faith?" When Christians have raised these kinds of questions, they have almost always concluded that the doctrine of the Trinity is a doctrine "by which the church stands or falls." This is a doctrine that we cannot do without, and understanding it better enriches our lives. The Trinity offers keys to a real and tangible difference in the way we understand ourselves, our God, and the way we live out our Christian faith.

Key to a Christian Reading of the Bible

The Trinity is the key to a Christian reading of the Bible. We have argued that the Bible demands the affirmation of the doctrine of the Trinity. This is a difficult doctrine that Christians did not just "cook up" to make things more mysterious for ourselves. If the Bible did not insist upon the doctrine of the Trinity and thrust it upon us by many, many passages, there would be no good reason to affirm it. But the truth of the matter is that the Bible demands that we affirm this doctrine. In fact, a Christian reading of the Bible is impossible without it.

> Form teams of two or three. Read Matthew 28:19. Discuss what this Scripture says to you about the contemporary relevance of the doctrine of the Trinity. How might you and your church heed this call of Jesus? What are you currently doing in your congregation? What might you do?

Jesus' "great commission" in Matthew 28:19 is the most emphatic assertion of the doctrine of the Trinity and its link to the life and faith of the church through the rite of Christian baptism. "And Jesus came and said: . . . 'Go therefore and make disciples of all nations, baptizing them in the name of the Father and of the Son and of the Holy Spirit." The doctrine of the Trinity is liturgically linked to baptism because baptism is about embracing Christ unto salvation, and it is impossible to talk about Jesus Christ and Christian salvation without bringing in the doctrine of the Trinity.

While the Christian church has always regarded Matthew 28:19 as an authentic saying of Jesus faithfully recorded by Matthew—the use of it in the *Didache* (ca. A.D. 96) was a good example of this—some contemporary scholars have suggested that this saying does not go back to the lips of the risen Christ but is, in fact, a later addition.[2] Two things should be said about this development; first, simply because this saying is unique to Matthew's Gospel and does not appear in the other Gospels is insufficient grounds to doubt its authenticity. Secondly, even if this saying is considered to be a textual addition by the early Christian community, this tells us that *they believed* the affirmation of the Trinity was so utterly consistent with the witness of Jesus Christ that he *could* have and *would* have made this affirmation. More to the point, however, is the recognition that the Christian affirmation of the doctrine of the Trinity does not hang upon one particular passage. The Trinity is woven deeply into the entire fabric of the New Testament.

A person cannot understand the authentic message of the Synoptic Gospels without coming to the conclusion of the Roman centurion in Mark's Gospel: "Truly this man was God's Son!" (Mark 15:39). This saying reflects upon the role of the Trinity. The message is even more predominant in John's Gospel, where Jesus openly declared his union with the Father in passages like "The Father and I are one" (John 10:30) and "Whoever has seen me, has seen the Father" (John 14:9). This same recognition stands behind the famous "I am" sayings of the Johannine tradition, most notably the one in John 8:58: "Very truly, I tell you, before Abraham was, I am." The "upper room discourses," in John 13–18, are completely unintelligible apart from a rudimentary understanding of the doctrine of the Trinity; how else can Jesus (the Son) speak of going to the Father and sending the Holy Spirit—as he does in Chapters 14 and 16? Jesus' "high priestly" prayer, in John 17, also stands on the foundation of the recognition of Jesus' union with the Father.

> Form three teams. Each team will read one of the following Scriptures: John10:30; John14:9; and John 8:58. How do these Scriptures inform your understanding of the relevance of the Trinity for contemporary Christians? Gather as one large group and share your insights with one another. Scan John 13–18 and choose verses that speak to you about the relevance of the Trinity for today. What are they? How do they speak to you?

In a similar way, Pauline passages like 2 Corinthians 13:13 show Paul's affirmation of the Trinity as well as its growing liturgical role in the life of the first-century church. Second Corinthians 13:13 includes a Trinitarian blessing: "The grace of the Lord Jesus Christ, the love of God, and the communion of the Holy Spirit be with all of you."

> Read 2 Corinthians 13:13. Write a paraphrase of this greeting that reflects your understanding of the Trinity. What does it say to you about the grace, love, and fellowship of God for contemporary Christians?

This passage also reflects the heart of Pauline theology. For Paul "the grace of the Lord Jesus Christ" and God's love are roughly synonymous because the love of God was emphatically shown to us through the life, death, and resurrection of Jesus Christ. Where God's grace and love are at work, in the community of faith, there is the "fellowship of the Holy Spirit." Other important Pauline passages, like 2 Thessalonians 2:13-14 and 1 Corinthians 12:4-6, express the Christian gospel of salvation in Trinitarian form. A host of Pauline passages contain hints or germinal assertions about the Trinity that were subsequently developed by Christian pastors and lay theologians, and a similar pattern could be traced in the other New Testament epistles as well.[3] Leonardo Boff rightly reminds us that this New Testament witness was so insistent that it created a "Christian re-reading of the Old Testament" that came to see Trinitarian "foreshadowing" in it as well.[4]

Key to Understanding God and God's Works

The Trinity is crucial to a Christian understanding of God and God's great works. One of the fundamental messages of the doctrine of the Trinity is that we serve and stand in relationship with a relational God. While it is difficult for us to fully comprehend the relationship that the Son enjoys with the Father, we know that it is analogous (to some degree) to human parent and child relationships. This is part of the theological impact of using language like "Father" and "Son" to describe the first and second persons of the Trinity. When we use Trinitarian language like this, we humans get a sense (though perhaps only a faint glimmer) of the love that exists within the Godhead. When Jesus described the Holy Spirit as "another Advocate" (John 14:16), he implied that the Holy Spirit and the Son of God enjoy a similar role and relationship with the Father. The doctrine of *perichoresis* teaches that each person of the Trinity shares mutually in the life of the others; Father, Son, and Holy Spirit share in the same nature, will, love, wisdom, power, and so forth. The concept of appropriation reminds us that what one person of the Trinity does, is owned by and could be ascribed to the others. Thus, we see our God revealed as a relational God, who enjoys deep and substantial fellowship within the Godhead and who also cherishes humans enough to

> Think about the doctrine of *perichoresis,* or the mutual sharing of life, nature, will, love, wisdom, and power among the three persons of the Trinity. How does this sharing inform your understanding of being in relationship with God?

make covenant with us, to save us from sin and death, and to invite us to share in this love and fellowship (John 17). God's love extends not only to us but also to the oppressed and to the outcasts, and God grows love in us by calling us to act in love toward all of God's people.

In a similar way, the Trinity is crucial to understanding God's great works in the world. Creation was, as we have seen, a Trinitarian event. The layering of John 1:1-5 over the Creation in Genesis 1, identifies the Word (second person of the Trinity) as the agent through whom Creation was made—the Word cooperated with the Creator (God the Father). The Spirit of God "was moving over the face of the waters" (Genesis 1:2, RSV). Paul, in Colossians 1:15-17, links the creating and sustaining work of God together and names Christ as the one through whom creation was made and in

> Read Genesis 1, John 1:1-5, and Colossians 1:15-17. What do these Scriptures say to you about creation? about God, Jesus, and the Holy Spirit? about how the Bible interprets God's ongoing work in creation today?

whom creation holds together. "He is the image of the invisible God, the firstborn of all creation; for in him all things in heaven and on earth were created . . . all things have been created through him and for him. He himself is before all things, and in him all things hold together." Whether we conceive of it in traditional terms, or through the new models developed by process theologians, God's work in our world is a Trinitarian work. We need to use this important lens as we try to discern God at work in our lives and our world.

Our redemption is, as we have seen, a Trinitarian event. The Father loved the Son and loved the world, so God sent his Son into the world so that we might have eternal life (John 3:16). Jesus' death on the cross was a "ransom" (Mark 10:45) that paid the price of our bondage to sin and death. His broken body and shed blood established a "new covenant" (Matthew 26:28 and footnote) for us based on forgiveness of sins through faith in him.

> How does the doctrine of the Trinity help you understand God's redemption? What does it mean to you to be a "new creation"?

The Son (with the Father) sends the Holy Spirit into our lives to convict us of sin and righteousness, to guide us into all truth, and to call to mind the things of Christ (John 16:12-15). Jesus promised, "You know him, because he abides with you, and he will be in you" (John 14:17). The work of the Holy Spirit within Christians is the "fruit of the Spirit" (Galatians 5:22-26), the growth of a Christian, Christ-like, character. It is in this sense that Paul says we are a new creation: "If anyone is in Christ, there is a new creation: everything old has passed away; see, everything has become new" (2 Corinthians 5:17). Apart from the doctrine of the Trinity we would not adequately understand or appreciate our redemption (justification) and the new life (sanctification) we have in Jesus Christ. God has acted *for* us as Father in Creation and in redemption. God has come among us to dwell *with* us, in the person of the Son, and God dwells *in* us by the power and presence of the Holy Spirit.

Key to Christian Worship and Experience

The Trinity is the key to Christian worship and experience. The most basic act of Christian devotion is prayer, and Christian prayer is a Trinitarian event. Matthew 6:9 tells us that Jesus taught his disciples to pray to God the Father. John 16:24 says that Jesus told the disciples to "ask" God for anything in Jesus' name. These Scriptures show us that we pray *to* the

> Read Matthew 6:9, John 16:4, and Romans 8:26-27. How do they inform your practice of prayer? How does your practice relate to the doctrine of the Trinity?

Father, *through* the intercession of God the Son. In a similar way Paul's letter to the church in Rome tells us that the Holy Spirit helps us pray: "Likewise the Spirit helps us in our weakness; for we do not know how to pray as we ought, but that very Spirit intercedes with sighs too deep for words. And God, who searches the heart, knows what is the mind of the Spirit, because the Spirit intercedes for the saints according to the will of God" (Romans 8:26-27).

The sacraments of our church are also acts of the Trinity. In Christian baptism we follow the practice that Jesus enjoined, "baptizing them in the name of the Father and of the Son and of the Holy Spirit" (Matthew 28:19). The deep and mysterious workings of the Lord's Supper also take on a Trinitarian dimension. We pray to and praise God the Father for giving God the Son for us as a redemption for our salvation; partaking of Jesus' broken body and shed blood, in the creatures of bread and grape juice, we are identifying ourselves with the death of the second person of the Trinity and accepting His death by faith as an atonement for our sin. This mysterious connection between the body and the blood, and the bread and wine, between Christ's death and our salvation, is made real and authentic to us by an act of the Holy Spirit—whose task it is to "testify" to Christ (John 15:26). The ritual says, "Pour out your Holy Spirit on us gathered here, and on these gifts of bread and wine. Make them be for us the body and blood of Christ, that we may be for the world the body of Christ, redeemed by his blood." We have seen how deeply the Trinity is

> What acts of worship speak most to you about the Trinity? How do they inform your understanding of God?

woven into the hymns of our tradition. The Trinity is also celebrated in our liturgical acts of praise. The familiar words of the Doxology say, "Praise God from whom all blessings flow; praise him, all creatures here below; praise him above, ye heavenly host; praise Father, Son, and Holy Ghost. Amen." From personal prayer and family devotions, to the sacraments and corporate worship, the Trinity is the key to Christian worship.

The Trinity is also the key to understanding Christian experience. Paul's letter to the Romans describes the "Abba experience" in which God's Spirit bears witness to our spirit that we belong to God: "You have received a spirit of adoption. When we cry, 'Abba! Father!' it is that very Spirit bearing witness with our spirit that we are children of God" (Romans 8:15-16; *see also* Galatians 4:6). Because we belong to Christ, by faith, God gives us the privilege of praying to him with the same directness and familiarity that Jesus enjoyed (Mark 14:36). The "witness of the Spirit" is that inner sense of belonging that the Holy Spirit creates within those who belong to God, and it is a feature of this profound relationship we enjoy with God through faith in Jesus Christ. John Wesley viewed this most foundational Christian experience as a work of the Trinity: "I know not how anyone can be a Christian believer till 'he hath' (as St. John speaks) 'the witness in himself'; till 'the Spirit of God witnesses with his spirit that he is a child of God'—that is, in effect, till God the Holy Ghost witnesses that God the Father has accepted him through the merits of God the Son—and having this witness he honours the Son and the blessed Spirit 'even as he honours the Father.' "[5]

The Trinity Is Indispensable for Speaking About God

We observed, at the outset of this study, how difficult it is to speak accurately of God. Quite often we find ourselves speaking of God by way of analogy, using something located completely in our frame of experience to express or to try to explain to someone who lives beyond the frame of our experience. We also have plenty of Scripture passages that use helpful human analogies; hence, the psalmist reports: "As a father has compassion for his children, / so the LORD has compassion for those who fear him" (Psalm 103:13), or again the Lord announces through the prophet Isaiah: "As a mother comforts her child, / so I will comfort you" (Isaiah 66:13). In each instance the care and concern that human fathers and mothers have toward their children supplies both language and analogy that accurately express God's attitudes and actions toward humans. Various types of parent metaphors have been employed by the mystics, poets, and hymn writers of the Christian tradition down through the ages. The medieval mystical writer, Julian of Norwich (ca. 1342–1423) used motherhood as a metaphor for understanding the life-giving and saving work of Jesus Christ.[6] In a similar way, we have observed that contemporary feminist writers opt for alternative metaphors for thinking of God; Sally McFague, for example, suggested Mother, Lover, and Friend as metaphors for the Trinity.[7] We have suggested that these new metaphors can be useful theologically if used and understood correctly.

But it is also important to distinguish, in our own minds, between *thinking about God* and *speaking to God*. That is to say, the metaphorical language that we use to envision and understand God may of necessity be different from the language of prayer and worship that we use to speak to God. Jesus could speak of his heavenly Father metaphorically, when trying to explain God to eager listeners (Matthew 6:26), and yet when he spoke to God he always addressed God as "Abba, Father." The language of prayer and worship may require more careful reflection than the language of sermon or song. For this reason, it is useful to point out that the

> What important implications does the doctrine of the Trinity hold for you and your Christian life? How do you think we should speak *about* God? How do you think we should speak *to* God?

Bible has repeatedly sanctioned the expressions of "Father, Son, and Holy Spirit" as accurate expressions for addressing God.

The reason that this sort of consideration matters and has some merit is because Jesus Christ enjoys a unique relationship with God the Father. The "Father-Son" language used in the traditional theology of the Trinity clearly points to that unique relationship (and not to maleness *per se*). In that regard, we should remind ourselves that the only time that Jesus used the phrase "Our Father" to address God the Father, was when he was responding to the disciples' request: "Lord, teach us to pray" (Luke 11:1). In all other instances, Jesus referred to God as "my Father" (Matthew 7:21; 10:32; 11:27; 16:17; Luke 10:22; and so on). In some instances he even took care to distinguish between "my Father" and "your father" (when referring to the Pharisees, John 8:38, 54, RSV). Trinitarian language is not only about our relationship with God, it is about the relationships of God within the Godhead. Hence, we need to be clear and careful in our own minds, whether we are speaking about God as God relates to us, or whether we are describing the nature of the Godhead. In my view, the doctrine of the Trinity helps us immeasurably when we are speaking about the nature and inner-relationships of God.

Closing

Stand, form a circle, and join hands. Sing stanza 1 of the hymn "Holy, Holy, Holy." Read the following Charles Wesley hymn in unison as a closing prayer:

1. He is our Life, the Lord our God:
   Our Father's love we find,
   Who being graciously bestow'd
   On us, and all mankind:
   Jesus our Life alike we own,
   Our Life eternal here
   Conceal'd, and by the world
        unknown;
   But He shall soon appear.

2. The Spirit is Life, we know and feel
   Who life to us imparts;
   And God doth in Three Persons dwell
   For ever in our hearts:
   Our Life is One: a Trinity
   In Unity we love,
   And gladly die from earth, to see
   His Face unveil'd above.[8]

Sing the Doxology as a closing for this session and this study of the Trinity.

Notes

1. Charles Wesley's *Hymns on the Trinity*, pages 94–95. The hymn can be sung to tunes like "Bealoth," used with the hymn "Spirit of Faith, Come Down"; "Diademata," used with the hymn "Crown Him with Many Crowns"; or "Terra Beata," used with the hymn "This Is My Father's World."

2. *Trinity and Society*, page 36.

3. Among these are: Galatians 3:11-14; 4:6; 2 Corinthians 1:21-22; 3:3; Romans 14:17-18; 15:16; 15:30; Philippians 3:3; Ephesians 2:18; 2:20-22; 3:14-17. *See Trinity and Society*, pages 38–39.

4. *Trinity and Society*, pages 40–42.

5. Outler, *JW Sermons,* II, page 385

6. James Walsh, trans. *Julian of Norwich: Showings* (New York: Paulist Press, 1978), chapters 55–56. Quoted in Tyson, ed. *Invitation to Christian Spirituality*, pages 193–95.

7. *Models of God*, pages 78–87.

8. Charles Wesley's *Hymns on the Trinity*, page 79. The hymn is based on Deuteronomy 30:20, Colossians 3:4, and Romans 8:10. It may be sung to tunes like "Carol" used with the hymn "It Came Upon a Midnight Clear"; "Cleansing Fountain," used with the hymn "There Is a Fountain Filled With Blood"; "Gerald," used with the hymn "I Want a Principle Within"; or "Materna," used with the hymn "America the Beautiful."

GLOSSARY

Appolinarianism: From Appolinarius (310–90) who taught that Jesus Christ's true humanity was comprised of body, soul, and spirit. While Jesus had a human body and soul, Appolinarius believed that Jesus had the logos (Word) of God as his spirit. This meant that Jesus Christ did not share the full humanity of all humans.

Appropriation: With respect to the Trinity, appropriation describes the way in which each person of the Trinity participates and owns the actions and works of the other members of the Holy Trinity. Hence, what is done by the Father can be said to be done by the Son and the Holy Spirit and vice versa.

Apocryphal: Literary works that were not accepted into the canonical Bible because they were deemed to be falsely attributed to apostolic writers and were deficient in their theological teaching.

Arians (Arianism): Followers of Arius (260–336), who did not believe in the full deity of Jesus Christ. They affirmed, rather, that Jesus was a creature who was not equal to God the Father, nor was Jesus eternal in the same way the Father is, and he did not share the same divine substance with God the Father.

Benediction: Literally, "good words." Prayers and blessings exchanged among Christians.

Cerinthianism: Followers of Cerinthius (ca.100–40), who accepted a metaphysical dualism in which matter was evil and spirit was good. For this reason they doubted that Jesus had a true human body, but rather was a spirit being who only seemed to have a physical, human body. *See* docetism.

Christology: The formal study of the aspects and ideas associated with Jesus Christ.

Docetism: Literally, "seems to." It describes an early Christological heresy that denied that Jesus Christ had true humanity and a real human body. Docetists argued that Jesus only "seemed to" have a true human body; actually his body was made of Spirit.

Ebionites: A sect of early Jewish Christians who did not accept the unique divinity of Jesus Christ because it was antithetical to Judaism.

Filioque clause: Literally, "and the Son." It was used to describe the Roman (or Latin) church's belief that the Holy Spirit proceeds or is sent to us by the Father and the Son. The Eastern Orthodox Church affirms that the Holy Spirit proceeds from the Father alone.

Gnostic(ism): Literally, "to know." It describes an early sectarian, synergistic religion that combined Christian and non-Christian ideas. The gnostic system of belief was based on the idea of salvation through secret knowledge. Hence, the gnostics were "knowers" of this secret knowledge.

Hermeneutics: The science of biblical interpretation and the study of principles and patterns of biblical interpretation.

Idolatry: The worship of idols, either literally or figuratively, through false ideas about God.

Immanent (Immanence): God as "up close and personal." The view of God as being immediately at hand, intimately involved in the world processes, and immediately accessible. The opposite of transcendence.

Incarnation: Literally, "taking flesh." It describes how, in the words of Scripture, "the Word became flesh and lived among us, ... full of grace and truth" (John 1:14).

Judaizers: Early Jewish Christians who sought to fit Christianity into the beliefs and practices of Judaism. This caused conflicts among the early Christians over matters like keeping the Jewish law and the divinity of Jesus.

Modalism: See monarchianism.

Monarchianism: A heretical view of the Trinity in which the Trinity was thought to go through three successive phases, first as Father, then as Son, and finally as the Holy Spirit, in a chronological progression. It was also called "modalism" because God goes through three separate and distinct modes of being.

Monotheism: The belief in and worship of only one God.

Nestorianism: From Nestorius (381–452), who viewed the humanity and divinity of Jesus Christ as being layered together as two separate identities rather than being integrated into an indissoluable, organic whole and union. This made Jesus seem like he was one-half god and one-half man, instead of very God and very man.

Perichoresis: Literally, "mutual interpretation." It describes the unique way that the Father, Son, and Holy Spirit share in each other's life, nature, thoughts, plans, aspirations, goals, and intentions. It describes a "community of being" in which the Trinity thinks, wills, plans, and acts in complete unity.

Person: With respect to the doctrine of the Trinity, *person* describes the threeness of the Trinity in terms of the relationship that exists between Father, Son, and Holy Spirit.

Polytheism: The belief in and worship of many gods.

Substance: The "oneness" of the Trinity expressed in terms of the Father, Son, and Holy Spirit each having the same significance for Christians.

Synoptic: Literally, "to see the same." Matthew, Mark, and Luke are described as the Synoptic Gospels because they (roughly) see the life of Jesus from a similar standpoint and present a similar story of Jesus in their respective Gospels.

Transcendent (Transcendence): God as "high and lifted up." The language of distance is used to express the recognition that God is above and beyond creation and our understanding of God; God is able to stand apart from the world as its Lord. The qualitative difference between Creator and creatures. The opposite of immanent/immanence.

Unitarianism: A radically monotheistic form of Christianity that rejects the doctrine of the Trinity and in so doing also denies the full divinity of Jesus Christ.

APPENDIX A:
THE NICENE CREED*

We believe in one God,
    the Father, the Almighty,
    maker of heaven and earth,
    of all that is, seen and unseen.

We believe in one Lord, Jesus Christ,
    the only Son of God,
    eternally begotten of the Father,
    God from God, Light from Light,
    true God from true God,
    begotten, not made,
    of one Being with the Father;
    through him all things were made.
    For us and for our salvation
        he came down from heaven,
        was incarnate of the Holy Spirit and the Virgin Mary
        and became truly human.
        For our sake he was crucified under Pontius Pilate;
        he suffered death and was buried.
        On the third day he rose again
        in accordance with the Scriptures;
        he ascended into heaven
        and is seated at the right hand of the Father.
        He will come again in glory

to judge the living and the dead,
and his kingdom will have no end.

We believe in the Holy Spirit, the Lord, the giver of life,
who proceeds from the Father and the Son,
who with the Father and the Son
is worshiped and glorified,
who has spoken through the prophets.
We believe in the one holy catholic and apostolic church.
We acknowledge one baptism
for the forgiveness of sins.
We look for the resurrection of the dead,
and the life of the world to come. Amen.

[1] This text is sometimes called the "Constantinoplian Creed" because of the addition of the paragraph on the Holy Spirit that took place there. The full Nicene Creed (from A.D. 325) was reaffirmed and accepted at the Council of Constaninople in 381. From *The United Methodist Hymnal*, 880.

APPENDIX B:
THE ATHANASIAN CREED*

Whosoever will be saved: before all things it is necessary that he hold the Catholic Faith: Which Faith except every one do keep whole and undefiled: without doubt he shall perish everlastingly. And the Catholic Faith is this: That we worship one God in Trinity, and Trinity in Unity; Neither confounding the Persons: nor dividing the Substance. For there is one Person of the Father: another of the Son: and another of the Holy Ghost. But the Godhead of the Father, of the Son, and of the Holy Ghost, is all one: the Glory equal, the Majesty coeternal. Such as the Father is: such is the Son: and such is the Holy Ghost. The Father uncreated: the Son uncreated: and the Holy Ghost uncreated. The Father incomprehensible: the Son incomprehensible: and the Holy Ghost incomprehensible. The Father eternal: the Son eternal: and the Holy Ghost eternal. And yet they are not three eternals: but one eternal. As also there are not three uncreated: nor three incomprehensibles, but one uncreated: and one incomprehensible. So likewise the Father is Almighty: the Son Almighty: and the Holy Ghost Almighty. And yet they are not three Almighties: but one Almighty. So the Father is God: the Son is God: and the Holy Ghost is God. And yet they are not three Gods: but one God. So likewise the Father is Lord: the Son Lord: and the Holy Ghost Lord. And yet not three Lords: but one Lord. For like as we are compelled by the Christian verity: to acknowledge every Person by himself to be God and Lord: So are we forbidden by the Catholic Religion: to say, There be three Gods, or three Lords. The Father is made of none: neither created, nor begotten. The Son is of the Father alone: not made, nor created: but begotten. The

Holy Ghost is of the Father and of the Son: neither made, nor created, nor begotten: but proceeding. So there is one Father, not three Fathers: one Son, not three Sons: one Holy Ghost, not three Holy Ghosts. And in this Trinity none is afore, or after another: none is greater, or less than another. But the whole three Persons are coeternal, and coequal. So that in all things, as aforesaid: the Unity in Trinity, and the Trinity in Unity, is to be worshiped. He therefore that will be saved, must thus think of the Trinity.

Furthermore it is necessary to everlasting salvation: that he also believe rightly the Incarnation of our Lord Jesus Christ. For the right Faith is, that we believe and confess: that our Lord Jesus Christ, the Son of God, is God and Man; God of the Substance of the Father; begotten before the worlds: and Man, of the Substance of his Mother, born in the world. Perfect God: and perfect Man, of a reasonable soul and human flesh subsisting. Equal to the Father, as touching his Godhead: and inferior to the Father as touching his Manhood. Who although he be God and Man; yet he is not two, but one Christ. One; not by conversion of the Godhead into flesh: but by taking of the Manhood into God. One altogether; not by confusion of Substance; but by unity of Person. For as the reasonable soul and flesh is one man: so God and Man is one Christ; Who suffered for our salvation: descended into hell: rose again the third day from the dead. He ascended into heaven, he sitteth on the right hand of the Father God Almighty. From whence he shall come to judge the quick and the dead. At whose coming all men shall rise again with their bodies; And shall give account for their own works. And they that have done good shall go into life everlasting: and they that have done evil, into everlasting fire. This is the Catholic Faith: which except a man believe faithfully, he can not be saved.

[2] From Philip Schaff, *The Creeds of Christendom*, 3 Vol. (New York: Harper & Brothers, 1932), II, pages 66–70.

APPENDIX C:
THE SYMBOL (OR CREED)
OF CHALCEDON*

We, then, following the holy Fathers, all with one consent, teach men to confess one and the same Son, our Lord Jesus Christ, the same perfect in Godhead and also perfect in manhood; truly God and truly man, of a reasonable soul and body; consubstantial with the Father according to the Godhead, and consubstantial with us according to the Manhood; in all things like unto us, without sin; begotten before all ages of the Father according to the Godhead, in these latter days, for us and for our salvation, born of the Virgin Mary, the Mother of God, according to the Manhood; one and the same Christ, Son, Lord, Only-begotten, to be acknowledged in two natures, inconfusedly, unchangeably, indivisibly, inseparably; the distinction of natures being by no means taken away by the union, but rather the property of each nature being preserved, and concurring in one Person and one Subsistence, not parted or divided into two persons, but one and the same Son, and only begotten, God the Word, the Lord Jesus Christ, as the prophets from the beginning [have declared] concerning him, and the Lord Jesus Christ himself has taught us, and the Creed of the holy Fathers has handed down to us.

[3] From Philip Schaff, *The Creeds of Christendom*, 3 Vol. (Grand Rapids: Baker Book House, reprint 1977) II, pages 62–63.